Ex Libris

The Meadowbrook School
of Weston

The Land and People of

ITALY

The Land and People of®
ITALY

by *David Travis*

HarperCollins*Publishers*

ACKNOWLEDGMENTS

Country maps by Philip Stickler / Stickler Cartography
Every effort has been made to locate the copyright
holders of all copyrighted materials and to secure
the necessary permissions from them. In the event that
any questions arise over credits and permissions,
the publisher will be glad to make necessary
changes in future printing and editions.
All photos not otherwise credited were taken by the author.

The Land and People of Italy
Copyright © 1992 by HarperCollins Publishers
Printed in the U.S.A. All rights reserved.
For information address HarperCollins Children's Books,
a division of HarperCollins Publishers,
10 East 53rd Street, New York, NY 10022.
1   2   3   4   5   6   7   8   9   10
First Edition

Library of Congress Cataloging-in-Publication Data
Travis, David, date
    The land and people of Italy / by David Travis.
        p.   cm. — (Portraits of the nations)
    Filmography: p.
    Discography: p.
    Includes bibliographical references (p.   ) and index.
    Summary: An introduction to the history, geography, economy,
culture, and people of Italy.
    ISBN 0-06-022778-8. — ISBN 0-06-022784-2 (lib. bdg.)
    1. Italy—Juvenile literature. [1. Italy.] I. Title. II. Series.
DG417.T73 1992   91-9771
945—dc20   CIP
                                                             AC

To Cristina Barbagli, my wife and global consultant

Contents

THE WORLD

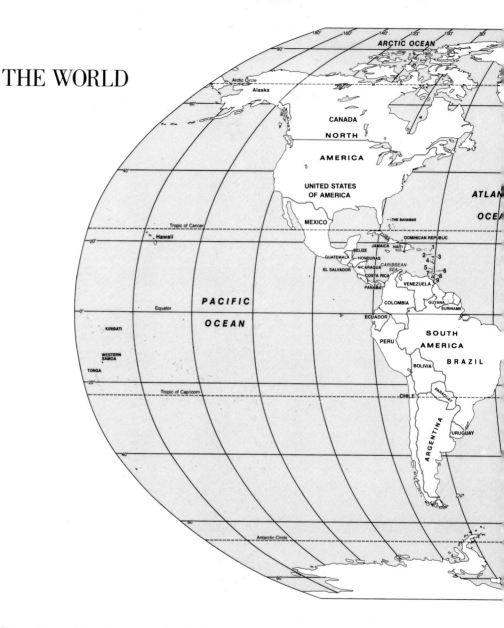

This world map is based on a projection developed by Arthur H. Robinson. The shape of each country and its size, relative to other countries, are more accurately expressed here than in previous maps. The map also gives equal importance to all of the continents, instead of placing North America at the center of the world. *Used by permission of the Foreign Policy Association.*

Legend

—— International boundaries

-------- Disputed or undefined boundaries

Projection: Robinson

0	1000	2000	3000 Miles

0	1000	2000	3000 Kilometers

Caribbean Nations

1. Anguilla
2. St. Christopher and Nevis
3. Antigua and Barbuda
4. Dominica
5. St. Lucia
6. Barbados
7. St. Vincent
8. Grenada
9. Trinidad and Tobago

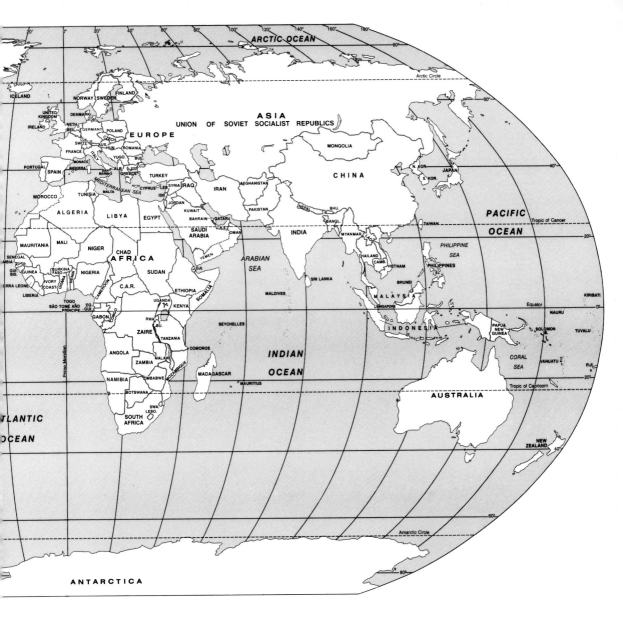

Abbreviations

ALB.	—Albania	C.A.R.	—Central African Republic	LEB.	—Lebanon	SWA.	—Swaziland
AUS.	—Austria	CZECH.	—Czechoslovakia	LESO.	—Lesotho	SWITZ.	—Switzerland
BANGL.	—Bangladesh	DJI.	—Djibouti	LIE.	—Liechtenstein	U.A.E.	—United Arab Emirates
BEL.	—Belgium	EQ. GUI.	—Equatorial Guinea	LUX.	—Luxemburg	YUGO.	—Yugoslavia
BHU.	—Bhutan	GER.	Germany	NETH.	—Netherlands		
BU.	—Burundi	GUI. BIS.	—Guinea Bissau	N. KOR.	—North Korea		
BUL.	—Bulgaria	HUN.	—Hungary	RWA.	—Rwanda		
CAMB.	—Cambodia	ISR.	—Israel	S. KOR.	—South Korea		

Mini Facts

OFFICIAL NAME: Republic of Italy *(Repubblica Italiana)*

LOCATION: A peninsula in southern Europe extending into the
Mediterranean Sea. Bounded by Slovenia and the Adriatic
Sea to the east, the Ionian and Mediterranean seas to the
south, the Tyrrhenian and Ligurian seas and France to the
west and Switzerland and Austria to the north.

AREA: 116,304 square miles (301,227 square kilometers)

POPULATION: 57,504,691 (1988)

PRINCIPAL CITIES: Rome (capital), Milan, Naples, Turin

ADMINISTRATION: Regions (20 total, 5 with special status); Provinces
(94); Communes (8,097)

LANGUAGES: Italian (with local dialects), French, German, Albanian,
Arabic

RELIGIONS: Catholicism, Protestantism, Judaism, Islam

TYPE OF GOVERNMENT: Republic, founded 1946

HEAD OF STATE: President of the Republic (7-year term)

HEAD OF GOVERNMENT: President of the Council of Ministers
(variable term)

PARLIAMENT: Senate (315 members) and Chamber of Deputies (630
members); legislative term is five years

POLITICAL PARTIES: Christian Democracy (DC), Democratic Party of
the Left (PDS—ex-Communist party), Socialist
Party (PSI), Italian Social Movement (MSI—neo-
Fascist), Republican Party (PRI), Social-
Democratic Party (PSDI), Italian Liberal Party
(PLI), Radicals (PR), Greens *(Verdi)*, Proletarian
Democracy (DP), regional and local parties,
special-interest parties

LITERACY RATE: 97.8% (1987)

MONETARY UNIT: Lira. Exchange rate (1992): Lire 1,200 = U.S. $1.00

MAIN PRODUCTS: *Agriculture*—almonds, cheese, fruits, grains, live-
stock, olives, wine, sugar beets, tobacco, potatoes

Industry—automobiles, marble, chemicals, clothing,
leather goods, machine tools

LIFE EXPECTANCY: Men, 70 years; Women, 76 years (1980)

Introduction: History Around Every Corner

Italy is a very young nation built on very ancient foundations. Civilization in Italy goes back more than two thousand years, and the idea of something called "Italy" is probably even older. The name "Italy" first appeared on the maps of the ancient Greeks. During the time of the Roman Empire, "Italy" meant the most advanced civilization in the Western world. Centuries later, in the 1500's, "Italy" stood for the beauty and splendor of Renaissance art and architecture. Italy, an old country, has a long history of civilization, power, and glory.

But Italy is also very young. Formed as a single nation only in 1861, Italy became a democracy, the Republic of Italy, in 1946, and a modern industrial country only in the 1960's. Today, the nation is thriving and

prosperous, the fifth richest in the world. Democracy is strong. Modern Italy is a young country, dynamic and well-known in the world.

The contrast between the young and the old, the very new and the very ancient, is part of the fascination of this country. The blend of modern and antique is seen every day and in almost every aspect of Italian life. A rock concert or a political demonstration shares the Piazza del Popolo (People's Square) in the capital city, Rome, with an ancient Egyptian obelisk (brought to Rome around 30 B.C.) and twin

Tourists walk behind one of the fountains at the Villa d'Este in Tivoli, near Rome. The series of fountains, pools, and waterfalls is a masterpiece of hydraulic engineering built in the 1500's. The waters flow through the garden of the powerful Este family's country home. UPI/Bettmann Newsphotos

churches (built in the late 1600's). Another obelisk and a magnificent column nearly two thousand years old stand in a square alongside the Italian Parliament. On the hottest summer evenings, the Romans converge on yet another downtown square, the Piazza Navona, to enjoy the fresh breeze and the open space. They walk on the same site where horses raced for the ancient emperors of Rome before A.D. 100.

There is the same blend of new and old in other Italian cities as well. People from around the world visit Florence and stroll through the city's main square, the Piazza della Signoria. The square is surrounded by masterpieces of early Renaissance architecture, but it lies on the ruins of an earlier medieval town that was itself built on top of an ancient Roman city. Italians and visitors alike flock to the small city of Verona, in the north, to enjoy opera on a moonlit summer night.

Sitting in the sun with coffee or ice cream, Italians watch the passing crowd in the Piazza Navona, originally built by the ancient Roman Emperors for horse racing. Agenzia Fotogiornalistica Cronaca Nuova/Carlo Bozzardi

The Walls of Rome

Surrounding the historic center of Rome are the city's magnificent walls. The Servian Wall, begun in 400 B.C., served to defend the original city. Little remains of this wall except for a few short sections. The Aurelian Walls, which date from A.D. 270, stretch for nearly 12 miles (19 kilometers) around the city and are mostly still standing.

The Walls are made of brick, the most common building material in ancient Rome. In some areas larger pieces of stone were used as well. The Walls are between 20 and 30 feet (6 and 9 meters) high. Guard towers stand along their length at regular intervals. Several gates allow entry into the city and are also the sites of many monuments and inscriptions that describe the conquests and glories of the past. Most of these gates carry the names of the wide streets built by the Romans to hold their empire together.

Shady and pleasant parks and even a museum are found alongside the Walls. A walk along the base of the Aurelian Walls is a nice introduction to the blend of ancient and modern in Italy. Crisscrossing through the entire city, the Walls tower over daily life, business affairs, and the city's chaotic traffic.

Twenty-five thousand people sip wine and soft drinks and listen to music that is a hundred years old while sitting in an ancient Roman amphitheater built two thousand years ago.

Hikers stumble across the past even in the isolated mountain areas of Italy. Trails follow the routes first established by ancient peoples who crossed the mountains to trade. Shepherds use the same paths too, moving their flocks to hillside pastures during the summer as they have done for centuries.

Opera on a summer's evening in the ancient Roman amphitheater in Verona. ENIT, Roma

There are so many signs of the past in Italy that they are often taken for granted. Ruins are sometimes disregarded and left abandoned. The great aqueducts, which once supplied the cities of ancient Rome with water, have mostly crumbled and fallen apart. A few of their magnificent arches still stand in the middle of the countryside, ignored by both the farmers who work in their shadows and the Italians who zoom by on the highways.

The past is not worshipped in Italy. Rather, it is the backdrop against which modern Italy goes about its business. This frequently means that the past is used in curious ways. The old, defensive walls of Italian cities have been hollowed out and converted into apartments. Shops have been built inside ancient arches, Roman temples made into churches, old theaters into restaurants. Some of today's freeways follow the same routes laid out by the Roman armies two thousand years ago.

The past is always present in Italy. But the past is much more than just background to modern life. The past is also a state of mind, and thousands of years of continuous civilization influence the way Italians view the world and think about themselves. They are a people deeply tied to their traditions and their past. Old ways of doing things are familiar and reassuring. Reluctant to adopt new ideas too quickly, the Italians change slowly and their society evolves gradually.

Italy: Pro and Con

The ruins and buildings of the past are only the most tangible signs of the many contributions that Italy has made to Western civilization over the past two thousand years. In politics, Italians developed both democracy and dictatorship. The Roman legal code was the basis of European justice for centuries. A tradition of superb art and architecture goes back to ancient Rome and continued into the Renaissance of the 1500's. Today's writers produce masterpieces of literature, as their forebears did before them. From da Vinci and Galileo to the present, some of the world's greatest scientists have been Italian. The country has excellent food and wine: Italy's Mediterranean diet is considered the world's healthiest. Rome has been the capital city of Catholicism, the largest Christian denomination, for centuries and is still the focus of attention for Catholics throughout the world.

Italy is a beautiful country, often called the "garden of Europe." It is a land of great variety, from tall mountains and icy streams in the north to the rocky, arid coastline of the south. It has gorgeous beaches facing the beautiful Mediterranean Sea as well as a peaceful and lush countryside lying near deeply forested mountains. Sunny and warm in the summer, Italy is one of the world's popular vacation spots.

Problems   Italy is also a country with many problems. Government is ineffective and slow to respond to changes in society. Scandals and corruption frequently trouble the Italian scene. Political patronage dominates the civil service and the economy, often resulting in poor policies that do not serve the nation's best interests.

Public services in Italy are inefficient. The post office, the national health care system, the tax bureau, and the railroad network are just a few examples of poor administration in some of the country's most important services.

Another serious matter is crime. Large areas of southern Italy are controlled by organized crime families such as the Mafia. The government is still unable to establish law and order in these regions.

Themes

History lies around almost every corner in every Italian town, whether large or small. And history will be found on almost every page of this book, because it is impossible to understand the present in a country with so much history without also understanding its past. The history section, alone five chapters in length, recounts the story of Italy from the most ancient peoples to the present. The weight and extent of history in Italy is one of the principal themes of this book.

A second theme is the Italians. Who are they, and what does it mean to be "Italian"? How has history contributed to the making of today's Italians?

The people of Italy are just as interesting as the land and its history. The Italians are universally known for their warmth and friendliness. They are generally an emotional people, able to smile and laugh with ease. They are also a social people who thrive on contact, interaction, and conversation with each other.

The Italians have exported their way of life and their attitudes throughout the world. As conquerors (the ancient Romans), as explorers (such as Christopher Columbus), and as poor immigrants looking for a better way of life, the Italians have traveled widely, introducing the many aspects of Italy and the outlook of its people to the rest of the world.

Finally, Italy is also a land of great variety. Though history is always present, it has taken many different forms in different areas of the country. For long periods of time, sometimes for hundreds of years, Italy has been a land divided into many separate countries, with different rulers, customs, and languages. Additionally, the geography and climate on the Italian peninsula vary widely from region to region. Geography and history have therefore combined to create many Italys within this one country. The variety is still seen today in the way Italians live, work, talk, and even eat. A third major theme in this book, then, is the variety of land and life in modern Italy.

A Tour of Rome

The capital city of Italy, Rome, is the best place to start in the exploration of Italy and its people. Visitors come to Rome in search of the city's ancient splendor. They have a surprise waiting for them: The modern city blends into the ancient one, making it impossible to see one without the other.

The living city of Rome moves at a hectic pace all day long and usually late into the night. Vast numbers of cars create traffic jams that begin early in the morning and last until long after dinnertime. Crossing the street often seems like a life-and-death adventure. The city is loud and chaotic. Honking horns settle unending problems of parking and right-of-way among Rome's drivers; voices fill the streets, negotiating the price of fruit and vegetables in open-air markets. Peace and tranquility are almost unknown in the city. Even the parks are full of par-

Heavy traffic is a problem the Italians face—and accept—as part of their daily lives in most of the country's large cities. Agenzia Fotogiornalistica Cronaca Nuova/Carlo Bozzardi

The River

Moving slowly through the center of Rome is the Tiber River (in Italian called the Tevere). The Tiber has figured in the history of Rome from the very beginning. The first inhabitants settled here because there was a shallow, year-round river crossing. Seven hills surrounded the site along the Tiber, providing protection. Salt flats stood nearby as well. As Rome grew, the Tiber become the city's connection to the sea, and small boats could sail as far up the river as Rome. Today, however, the Tiber is little used. The river sits far below street level and is hidden by walls built to control its autumn floods. Its banks are a surprisingly peaceful oasis in the middle of the hectic city.

ents and children, enjoying what few open spaces are to be found.

The ancient ruins are hidden amidst the bustle and noise of the modern city. The Forum, where Rome was founded, still displays the signs of its ancient status as the business, government, and religious center of a world empire. Nearby are the Colosseum and the Circus Maximus, two of the largest outdoor sports stadiums in the world, both constructed around two thousand years ago. The old walls built to defend Rome still encircle the city, and the Italians cross under them several times in a day. The crumbled remains of the Roman baths and the foundations of the old palaces of the emperors are also part of the cityscape.

The chaos and confusion of the capital city is uniquely Roman. Elsewhere the past blends with the present in softer and quieter ways. Throughout Italy the sight of so much history in a modern country is both intriguing and startling. The Italians rub shoulders with their history each and every day in this land where the past is always present.

The Boot in the Mediterranean

Italy is a long and narrow country that looks like a boot. The top of the boot rests in Europe, and the toe reaches almost to Africa, making Italy a land bridge between these two very different worlds. The fourth largest country in Western Europe (after France, Spain, and united Germany), Italy's total land area of about 116,000 square miles (just over 300,000 square kilometers) makes the country about the same size as the state of Arizona (and only one thirtieth the size of the United States).

There is an extraordinary variety of land forms and climates in Italy. In the north are Europe's tallest mountains, while the south has hot and arid plains. In between lie many little Italys, each one with a different appearance and different climate. Despite the regional variation in

Italy, two features are most important in understanding its geography: the seas and the mountains.

The Sea

Italy is a peninsula that sticks out more than 700 miles (approximately 1,150 km.) into the middle of the Mediterranean Sea. The sea surrounds Italy on three sides, creating an enormous coastline of about 6,000 miles (10,000 km.). The water is always nearby, and the Italians have been drawn to the sea from the earliest times. The major port cities of Italy (Genoa, Naples, Venice, and Trieste) have histories that

Encircled on three sides by the sea, the Italians have always been ocean travelers. This is Portofino, the most popular port for private boats on the Gulf of Genoa. Superstock

Above the chaotic and crowded center of Naples stand beautiful villas with views of the city and the bay. Magnum

go back hundreds of years. Most Italians still live in villages or cities near the coast.

The peninsula of Italy divides the eastern half of the Mediterranean Sea from the western half. Directly in the path of all travelers on the Mediterranean, Italy has been a stopping-off point for many different peoples from the very beginning of its recorded history.

The Mediterranean Sea divides Italy from its closest African neighbors: Tunisia and Libya. The Mediterranean around Italy is itself divided into four smaller seas. The Ligurian Sea lies in the northwest and includes the Gulf of Genoa. The Tyrrhenian Sea, west of Italy, separates the mainland from the large Italian island of Sardinia (Corsica belongs to France). The Tyrrhenian reaches south to the tip of the

PHYSICAL FEATURES

0   50   100 miles
0   50   100   150 km

Alps
BRENNER PASS
Dolomite Alps
Maritime Alps
Lake Maggiore
Lake Lugano
Lake Como
Milan
Lake Garda
Po River
Trieste
Venice
Gulf of Venice
Genoa
Bologna
LIGURIAN SEA
Florence
Arno River
Lake Trasinero
Elba Island
Corsica
Tiber River
Lake Bracciano
Rome
Apennines
ADRIATIC SEA
Sardinia
Tyrrhenian Sea
Naples
Ischia
Mount Vesuvius
Capri
Gulf of Taranto
Mediterranean Sea
Lipari Islands
Ionian Sea
Palermo
Sicily
Mount Etna
Pantelleria

Italian boot. A narrow channel, the Straits of Messina, separates Sicily from southern Italy. The Ionian Sea lies to the south. It is one of the deepest seas in the Mediterranean, extending down to nearly 16,000 feet (4,900 meters). Underneath the "heel" of the Italian boot is the Gulf of Taranto. The fourth sea is the Adriatic, off the east coast. The

Adriatic Sea is a long, narrow body of water between Italy and the nations of the former republic of Yugoslavia. Unlike the Ionian, the Adriatic is quite shallow, averaging only 650 feet (200 meters) in depth.

Scattered throughout the four Italian seas of the Mediterranean are a number of islands. The two largest are Sardinia and Sicily. Off the northwestern coast is the island of Elba (rich in minerals and best known as the prison of Napoleon in 1814). Farther south in the Tyrrhenian Sea are the islands of Ponza, Ischia, and Capri (a famous resort). Ustica and the seven Lipari Islands (in Italian, the Isole Eolie) lie north of Sicily, while to the south, Pantelleria and Lampedusa are the Italian islands closest to the African nation of Libya. A larger island, an independent country called the Republic of Malta, sits in the Mediterranean Sea, 60 miles (97 km.) off the southern coast of Sicily.

The Mountains

Surrounded by the sea, Italy is also crisscrossed by mountains. In the north, where the Italian boot is anchored to Europe, are the Alps. A long chain of mountains, the Alps extend for over 900 miles (1,500 km.) in a curving, concave arch. The peaks of the Alps are extremely high. Mont Blanc's summit is the tallest at 15,771 feet (or 4,807 meters); Mount Rosa, another high peak, reaches to 15,220 feet (4,639 meters). Most of the other mountaintops are between 8,000 and 11,500 feet (2,500 to 3,500 meters). The Alps divide northern Italy from the neighboring countries of France (to the west), Switzerland and Austria (to the north), and Slovenia (to the east).

In the past the Alps acted as a natural barrier between Italy and

This small, family-run grocery store on the Lipari Islands north of Sicily is typical of rural, southern Italy. Susan Meyers

Mount Cristallo, 10,551 feet (3,216 meters), towers above a mountain valley near the resort town of Cortina, in the Dolomite Alps of northeastern Italy.   Envision

central Europe. This formidable chain of mountains encouraged the Italians to look to the seas for transportation because there were very few places to cross the Alps, especially in the winter, when the snows covered the mountains. The lowest-lying point, at 4,400 feet (1,350 meters), is the Brenner Pass, which connects Italy and Austria. The Brenner has been an important trade route for thousands of years, and armies have crossed this pass on their way to war over the centuries. In the last hundred years several tunnels have been carved through the Alps. These have made travel between Italy and Europe much easier all year round. The most important of these tunnels is the one under Mont Blanc, connecting Italy to France; it is 9 miles (15 km.) long.

San Marino

High in the Apennines is a nation that lies completely within Italy—the Republic of San Marino. This is a tiny, independent country that sits above the Adriatic Sea in eastern Italy. San Marino is the last surviving city-state from the Renaissance period. The Republic's constitution dates back to 1600. The area was first settled much earlier, in the fourth century, when a small group of Christians fled into the hills to escape religious persecution by the Romans. San Marino has a population of only 22,000 and a total area of less than 25 square miles (65 square km.). The Republic has close ties with Italy in virtually every field: The official language is Italian, the principal religion is Catholicism, and the country's currency is the Italian lira. The government is led by two regents, chosen by the Great and General Council of Representatives for six-month terms. The three major political parties in San Marino—the Communists, the Socialists and the Christian Democrats—are each closely tied to their counterparts in Italy.

The chief economic activities in San Marino are tourism and the sale of the Republic's postage stamps to collectors throughout the world. Small farms provide some of the food for the population, and there is limited light industry. But San Marino's well-being is dependent on the economy of Italy, the nation that surrounds this mountaintop Republic on all sides.

Glaciers still exist on the high slopes of the northern Alps. Many signs of glacial activity in Italy's distant past remain today. The four "great lakes" in the north—Maggiore, Lugano, Como, and Garda—are all the result of glaciers descending out of the Alps in prehistoric times.

A second chain of mountains, the Apennines, runs down the center of Italy for 300 miles (500 km.). From the northwest near the Gulf of Genoa all the way to Sicily, the Apennines divide the peninsula between east and west. The highest point on the Apennines is in the center of Italy at the Grand Sasso mountain, whose altitude is 9,558 feet (2,914 meters).

The Apennines are an extremely rugged chain with deep canyons and steep slopes. Historically, the Apennines made travel quite difficult throughout the peninsula. Until recently, the small villages of the mountains were isolated from each other, and they developed on their own with relatively little contact with the rest of the world. The result has been the creation of many different pockets of culture and tradition, almost miniature nations, within the mountains.

Earthquakes and Volcanoes

There is quite a bit of geological activity throughout the Apennines. Deep below the earth's surface, the foundations of the mountains are moving slowly to the northeast. Earthquakes are the result of this underground movement. Tremors are common in Italy, and some of these have been quite devastating. The most recent was a serious earthquake that rocked the southern Apennines in 1980, destroying many villages and leaving thousands of people homeless.

Italy also has extensive volcanic activity. There are four active volcanoes in the country. Mount Vesuvius dominates the Bay of Naples, and the volcanoes of Stromboli and Vulcano form two of the Lipari Islands off the northern coast of Sicily. Mount Etna, in Sicily, is Italy's largest and most active volcano. Etna rises to nearly 10,500 feet (3,200 meters), and during the winter it is a popular ski area. The volcano last erupted in 1991, spilling lava down its southeast slope toward the city of Catania.

Several large lakes in central Italy are also the result of volcanic activity. Lake Trasimeno and Lake Bracciano are both volcanic craters that have filled with water. Natural springs, common throughout Italy, are yet another sign of geological activity. Water for the city of Rome comes mostly from such springs. Near the small village of Tivoli in the central Apennine Mountains, the natural springs were used to create a marvelous garden of fountains in the sixteenth century.

The Alps and the Apennines account for 35 percent of all the land area of Italy. Foothills account for another 40 percent of the land. Much of Italy, then, is mountainous. This means that only a relatively small part of the country (less than one quarter) is suitable for agriculture or large cities.

Rivers

Because of its many mountains, Italy has only a few large rivers. The longest is the Po. The Po River drains the enormous valley enclosed by the Alps and the Apennines. Beginning in the high mountains on the French border, the Po flows eastward for over 400 miles (650 km.) to the Adriatic Sea. Some of the most fertile agricultural land in all Italy is found along its banks. Two of the country's most important industrial cities, Turin and Milan, are found in the valley formed by the Po River.

The Tiber River carries water from the central Apennines first southward and then west to the Tyrrhenian Sea, passing through Rome. The third important river of Italy is the Arno, which drains the central Apennines to the north and west. The Arno River flows through the cities of Florence and Pisa before reaching the northern Tyrrhenian Sea near Livorno.

The Po, Tiber, and Arno are all northern rivers. There are fewer rivers in the south because of the drier climate. And unlike northern rivers, which are fed by snowmelt and rainfall, southern rivers do not have a steady flow of water. In the south, rivers flood during the winter and dry up during the summer.

Climate

Most people think of Italy's climate as sunny and warm. But pleasant year-round weather is found only in a few places on the peninsula, such as the Gulfs of Genoa and Naples, the Amalfi coast, the inland area near Rome, and the island of Sicily. In the rest of Italy, the climate is more severe and the weather is subject to rapid changes, determined

With its hot, dry climate and poor soil, southern Italy is a difficult land for agriculture. Here, on a Sicilian farm near Ragusa, almond trees stand over a field ready for vegetables. The trees provide some needed shade and the pockets gather all the water possible. Thomas Roma

by the interplay between the sea and the mountains. The Mediterranean Sea and the Alps and Apennines create great instability and wide variability in the country's weather.

Temperatures vary on the peninsula. The really hot areas lie south of Rome, as one gets closer to Africa. Inland areas of Sicily easily reach 100° Fahrenheit (38° Centigrade) during the hottest months of July and August; it is rare to find such high temperatures north of Rome. The southern coastal areas remain cooler, at 80°F (27°C). This is the same average summer temperature as Rome, but higher than the normal temperatures in the north, which average 75°F (24°C). In the winter, the average temperature in the north is only 35°F (2°C), while in the south the winters are more mild, with temperatures averaging around 48°F (9°C).

Precipitation, too, varies widely in Italy. The Alps and Apennines receive most of the rain and snow. The areas south and east of the mountains receive much less precipitation during the year. And the farther south one travels, the less rain and snow falls. Some areas of the south go without any rain whatsoever for three or four months in the summer. On the other hand, most of the north of Italy has at least a little rain all year, with particularly intense storms in the spring and fall. Thunderstorms and torrential downpours occur frequently in the central areas of Italy. In general, northern Italy has a wet and cool climate. Southern Italy is hotter and drier, more like Africa, which is nearby.

Much of the north, particularly the Po River Valley, has dense fog for most of the winter. Though the moisture is good for farming, the fog makes driving hazardous and closes many of Italy's airports for several days at a time from November to February.

Winds are another aspect of the peculiar climate in Italy. Temperature differences between the land and the sea often create very strong winds. Hot and dry winds blow their way north from Africa into southern Italy during the summer. These are called the *scirocco*, and they carry sand from the African deserts with them. The day after a *scirocco*, windows, balconies, and cars as far north as Rome are covered with a fine layer of gray sand blown into Italy from the Sahara Desert 1,500 miles (2,400 km.) away. In the north, strong winds frequently sweep out of the eastern Alps and blow down into the Adriatic Sea, passing right through the city of Trieste. These winds are called the *bora*, and they can reach speeds of 100 miles (160 km.) an hour, making it dangerous even to walk outside. During the winter months, strong winds also buffet the Apennines. A weather station located at Mount Cimone in the Apennines has recorded winds of over 125 miles (200 km.) an hour.

North, Center, and South

The vast differences in both geography and climate throughout the peninsula make it difficult to speak of a single Italy. Instead, the country is commonly divided into three major areas—the North, the Center, and the South—each of which has its own characteristics. Northern Italy includes the land drained by the Po River as well as the area of the Ligurian Sea. Graced with the most fertile land and the most consistent supply of water, northern Italy is the country's most productive agricultural area. The North also has most of the nation's industries.

The central region of Italy includes the lands along the Arno and Tiber rivers as well as the western, Tyrrhenian shore and the eastern, Adriatic coast of Italy. The Center is a mostly mountainous region, with fewer and smaller plains dedicated to agriculture.

The South begins in the area around the port city of Naples and continues down to the tip of the peninsula. Sicily and Sardinia, the two large islands, are also part of southern Italy. Most of the South is mountainous and dry. The land is relatively poor, and rainfall is scarce.

Agriculture is much less productive here than in the North. The South has little industry.

The People on the Land

Who are the Italians on the peninsula? The current population is just under 57 million people. Italy's population is the second largest in western Europe (behind Germany's). Population density—the number of people per square mile—in Italy is high: 492 per square mile (1,274 per square km.), compared to 62 (160) in the United States.

There are more women in Italy (52 percent of the total) than men (48 percent). The country has one of the lowest birthrates in the world—less than two children (currently 1.8) for each couple. This means that Italy's population is not growing. Should the low birthrate continue, Italy's population may actually decrease by over 10 million in the next forty years.

Italy's Regions

North	*Center*	*South*
Emilia-Romagna	Lazio	Abruzzi
Friuli-Venezia Giulia	Marches	Basilicata
Liguria	Tuscany	Calabria
Lombardy	Umbria	Campania
Piedmont		Molise
Trentino-Alto Adige		Puglia
Valle d'Aosta		Sardinia
Veneto		Sicily

Nearly half of Italy's 57 million inhabitants live in the North (45 percent), while the Center has 20 percent of the population and the South 35 percent. For administrative purposes, Italy is divided into twenty regions. Each region is split into a number of smaller provinces (ninety-four in all of Italy), and each province is further divided into towns (called communes).

Italy is a country of villages and small towns. A slight majority of the Italians (51 percent) live in rural areas, and one third of the population lives in communes of less than ten thousand people. Most of Italy's eight thousand communes are quite small, with fewer than three thousand inhabitants each. Less than 2 percent of the communes are large cities (with more than fifty thousand people) and even the biggest Italian cities are relatively small: Rome (whose population is 3 million), Milan (1.5 million), Naples (1.2 million), Turin (1 million), Palermo and Genoa (each with just over 700,000 inhabitants).

The country's principal language is Italian. However, there are many different versions of Italian, called dialects, spoken throughout the country. Other languages are also spoken in Italy today. German is the most common in the northern area called Trentino-Alto Adige, near the Austrian border. There is a French-speaking population in the valleys of the Alps in northwestern Italy. People speaking Albanian live in parts of the south of Italy and on the island of Sicily as well. The inhabitants of the island of Sardinia also have their own language.

Most Italians are Catholics, though there are also small populations of Protestants and Jews. Immigrants from Africa have created an Islamic community as well.

Sheep graze on pastures underneath a deeply furrowed hill already prepared for spring planting. Near Asciano in Tuscany, not far from Siena. Magnum/Bruno Barbey

Immigration

Over the last ten years, there has been a dramatic increase in the number of immigrants coming to Italy. Nearly 1.5 million people have arrived from some of the poorest countries in the world. The majority of these immigrants come from Africa and Asia. How these new Italians are faring is discussed in Chapter IX.

The Italian peninsula continues to act as a bridge, connecting Africa with Europe and providing access for the poorer peoples of the Third World to the wealthier nations of Europe.

Ancient Peoples

Who were the first people to live on the Italian peninsula? Experts believe these first inhabitants, the true natives of Italy, came from three different groups. All three were Indo-European peoples, which means they originally came from central Europe and southern Russia, and had shared, ages earlier, a single common language.

The "Italian" Peoples

The first inhabitants were the so-called "Italian" peoples of the peninsula, who arrived from the north or east by 4000 B.C. Two thousand years later, they had divided into separate tribes. There were ten or twelve of these tribes, living in different regions of Italy. The principal ones were the Ligurians (near Genoa), the Veneti (in the flat plains behind the modern-day city of Venice), the Italics (including the Latins

Problems of Prehistory

The earliest signs of civilization in Italy date back more than six thousand years, but we know very little about these first Italians or their cultures. The civilizations in Italy prior to 1000 B.C. are part of the prehistory of the peninsula. Recounting the prehistory of any people is a very difficult and uncertain task. There are virtually no written records (often because there was no written language), only markings and designs. The reconstruction of the lives of such ancient people is based on mere fragments of their civilization—pieces of their pottery and tools.

Most of the prehistoric peoples of Italy disappeared. Absorbed or conquered by those who arrived later on the peninsula, many ancient Italians left little behind to testify to their existence. This further complicates the reconstruction of their societies. Our understanding of the original peoples is quite incomplete. The gaps in the past make prehistory a field in which many different theories are put forward to explain who the earliest Italians were, where they came from, and what their lives were like.

A nuraghe, *a construction of a prehistoric Sardinian people whose origins are still a mystery. This population was already present in the third century B.C. when the first Phoenician traders landed on the island. The* nuraghi *are thought to have marked the territory of a tribe and may have been used to defend the land in times of war. There are over 7,000 on Sardinia.* ENIT, Roma

and Sabines, both of whom lived in the area around Rome), the Umbrians (in central Italy), and the Sicles (on Sicily). The regions of Italy are named after these tribes, and the name *Italy* itself comes from these people, who considered themselves the sons of the bull god and called themselves the *vituli*. All these tribes lived in small villages; most were shepherds and engaged in simple agriculture.

Terramare and Villanova

Also included among the original inhabitants were the people of the *Terramare* (meaning "dark soil") civilization. These people moved across the Alps from central Europe around 2000 B.C., and settled in marshy areas of the Po River Valley. The houses of their small villages stood on platforms raised above the ground to protect them from flooding. They, too, lived off agriculture and shepherding, though the people of the Terramare also developed a simple textile industry using the wool of their sheep. They were probably the first people in Italy to work with iron and to use metal tools extensively.

The third "native" group in Italy in prehistoric times were the people of the Villanova culture. The name "Villanova" comes from the area near the city of Bologna where remnants of this civilization were first discovered. Like the Terramare, the Villanova people also settled first in the Po River Valley. No one is quite sure if the Villanova arrived from central Europe by sea or whether they developed out of a fusion of the Terramare with local tribes in the Apennine Mountains. They were good farmers and skilled workers in bronze. Their first settlements, only small villages, soon grew into substantial towns: Bologna, Tarquinia, and Veio are all thought to have been founded by the Villanova. Their civilization flourished in Emilia and later in all of central Italy, spreading south to Rome and eventually even into

ANCIENT PEOPLES
OF ITALY

0   50   100   150 miles
0   50   100   150   200 km

CELTS

LIGURIANS

UMBRIANS

ETRUSCANS

SABELLIAN
AND OSCAN
MOUNTAIN TRIBES

OSCAN
SAMNITES

LATIN STATES

APULIAN
OSCANS

MESSAPIANS

LUCANIAN

OSCANS

BRUTTIAN OSCANS

PHOENICIAN
SPHERE

GREEK
SPHERE

SICELS &
SICANIANS

SICILY   GREEK SPHERE

Campania. In the many areas where the Villanova and Terramare people overlapped, the earlier Terramare civilization was absorbed into
that of the Villanova.

· 33 ·

Apparently, the Villanova people did not establish a settlement at Rome, even though the location was ideal for a village. There was an easy crossing of the Tiber River and a well-established trail leading to nearby salt flats. Seven hills surrounded the swampy riverbanks, offering dry land and some form of defense. No one knows why the Villanova disregarded this prime site.

The Terramare and the Villanova peoples were the first Italians on the peninsula. But Italy's position in the middle of the Mediterranean Sea insured that others would soon visit the peninsula. Between 1000 and 700 B.C., peoples from the eastern Mediterranean explored the western areas of the sea, including the Italian peninsula. Many just stopped off, but some decided to stay, to trade, and to found colonies. Two such "foreign" peoples were of particular importance: the Phoenicians and the Greeks.

Phoenicians

The Phoenicians were originally from the Middle East, the present-day country of Lebanon and areas of western Syria. For several hundred years from 1200 B.C. onward, the Mediterranean was a Phoenician sea: The Phoenicians were the world's greatest traders and travelers. Moving into the central Mediterranean sometime around 1000 B.C., the Phoenicians founded many cities. Their most important settlement was Carthage, established on the shores of northern Africa (near the present-day country of Tunisia) around 800 B.C.

Particularly important to the oceangoing Phoenicians were the Straits of Messina, the narrow water passage between Sicily and the southern mainland of Italy. Sicily soon became a major outpost for the Phoenicians, who founded settlements on the west coast (Trapani) and the north coast (Palermo and Messina) of the island. They also established a village at Cagliari, on the island of Sardinia.

Greeks

A few centuries after the Phoenicians, the Greeks expanded their trade into new areas of the western Mediterranean. Between 700 and 600 B.C., several of the Greek city-states established outposts and colonies in two areas of Italy. In Calabria (the toe of the Italian boot) and Campania, the Greeks founded at least fifteen major cities, including Naples ("new town" in Greek), Reggio, and Cuma. The Greeks spread rapidly through the southern mainland, including the shores of the Gulf of Taranto and much of Puglia. The south of Italy was known in Latin as *Magna Grecia*, or "Greater Greece."

Written Language

The Phoenicians were the first international merchants of the Mediterranean. Their trading outposts spread from the Middle East to Spain. Their explorations eventually took them out of the Mediterranean along the Atlantic shore of Europe and even all the way around Africa.

The importance of trade to the Phoenicians led to the invention of a written language and an alphabet. The details of trade agreements needed to be recorded in an accurate and permanent fashion. A written language arose as a result.

The Phoenician script developed far beyond the earlier picture signs of Egyptian hieroglyphics and the wedge-shaped symbols of the cuneiform writings. The Phoenician's alphabet served as the foundation for virtually all the other writing systems in the Mediterranean. Written language not only allowed the Phoenicians to carry out business but it also gave the Mediterranean and European world the ability to save knowledge and pass it down from generation to generation. Few developments have been so important in human history.

Magna Grecia

"Greater Greece," established in Italy between the seventh and fifth centuries B.C., was really a series of trading outposts and colonies along the coastline. The Greeks dominated a coastal strip that was rarely more than 6 miles (10 km.) wide. The native populations inland sometimes traded with the Greeks (in Sicily) and sometimes fought them for territory (on the southern mainland of Italy).

Whether hostile or friendly to the Greeks, the native peoples of Italy picked up elements of this foreign culture. They gradually incorporated Greek metallurgy, pottery, burial traditions, and even religion into their own way of life. Later, as Rome expanded throughout the peninsula and dominated the native tribes after 500 B.C., these aspects of the Greek way of life became part of Italian civilization.

The Greeks also settled in Sicily, especially on the east coast (Catania and Syracuse) and along the southern shore (Agrigento). The Greek settlements in Sicily alarmed the Phoenicians, and many battles for control of the island took place between 500 and 250 B.C.

The Greeks brought the Western world's most advanced civilization with them when they arrived in Italy. They imported their religion and social customs; thus the integration of Greek culture with the native civilization of the first Italians in the South began.

The arrival of the Greeks and Phoenicians marked the end of the prehistoric epoch in Italy. These two civilizations, the major trading cultures and most powerful nations in the Mediterranean world, incorporated Italy and its original inhabitants (especially the tribes of the south and Sicily) into their empires. Italy was no longer culturally, economically, or politically isolated and left on its own.

Etruscans

The Greeks did not move out of the south of Italy, because another people blocked their efforts to expand northward. These were the Etruscans. No one knows much about the origins of the Etruscans, and their civilization remains something of a mystery. They are not considered an Indo-European people, because their language (as poorly as it is understood today) was entirely different from those of the other inhabitants of Italy, including the Greeks and the Phoenicians. Some experts believe that the Etruscans came from western Asia (from the area near Turkey); others maintain that they migrated across the Alps; a third group contends that the Etruscans developed out of a prehistoric Italian tribe whose traces have yet to be discovered. Whatever their

The Etruscans decorated their tombs with magnificent sculptured sarcophagi, including this one of a couple buried together. Museo Nazionale di Villa Giulia, Rome. EPT, Roma

origins, the Etruscans appeared in central Italy, in the region of Tuscany, between 1200 and 1000 B.C. They soon became the dominant civilization in that area.

The Etruscans built their first cities near the coast, just inland from the sea, overlooking rich agricultural lands. All their towns, fortified by massive walls, had regular city plans and were equipped with well-constructed streets and even sophisticated drainage and sewer systems. Around 800 B.C., the Etruscans expanded into central Italy, away from the Tyrrhenian Sea. They eventually founded twelve major towns in Tuscany (which means "the land of the Etruscans"), including Arezzo, Chiusi, Perugia, and Volterra (which was an enormous city with nearly 10 miles (16 km.) of walls and a population of almost 100,000 people). The Etruscans also moved southward out of Tuscany and into Lazio. Around 700 B.C., they established their own village at Rome, which soon dominated the original Latin settlement. The Etruscans then expanded into the Campania region and later headed northward, over the Apennines and into the area around Bologna.

Mixing Cultures
Wherever the Etruscans went, they assimilated with the existing peoples, mixing their way of life with those of the native tribes. The blend of many cultures and traditions made the Etruscan civilization a very rich one. From its very beginnings Italy had a complex and heterogeneous culture, which often drew on elements of some of the most advanced civilizations of its time.

The Etruscans reached the height of their power and influence in Italy between 550 and 500 B.C. They were an especially skilled people. Experts in working with metals, the Etruscans mined iron, zinc, tin, lead, copper, and bronze. The island of Elba in the Tyrrhenian Sea served as their mine, and the forests of Tuscany provided the wood to fuel their metallurgy. The Etruscans were also good farmers who improved their lands with irrigation and drainage canals.

Etruscan craftsmen excelled in detailed gold work and jewelry, bronze mirrors, and statues; the production of elegant terra-cotta vases, leather goods, and textiles; and even the construction of false teeth. Most importantly, the Etruscans traded all their goods throughout Europe. Etruscan products have been found not only in northern Italy but over the Alps and along the Rhone and Rhine rivers into France, Switzerland, and Germany. Like the Phoenicians and the Greeks, the Etruscans also brought Italy out of isolation by trading throughout the world.

Life in Etruscan Italy

Each Etruscan city was initially ruled by a single monarch who held absolute power. As trade increased and the Etruscans prospered, power was divided among the richest families of each city, and a wealthy aristocracy came to govern the cities of Etruscan Italy. The symbol of political power was an axe tied into a bundle of rods, called the *fasces*. Each Etruscan town was independent of the others, although they formed loose alliances in case of war.

The Etruscans were skilled artists. Both men and women attended school and studied. Indeed, most Etruscan art shows men and women engaged in the same activities; there appears to have been very little difference in the social roles of the two sexes. Leisure time was spent in sports, including boxing, javelin, discus, bull-fighting, and dice games.

The glue that held the Etruscan civilization together was its religion. The Etruscans worshipped nature. They believed in many gods and goddesses, whose wishes they understood by reading divine signs—in the stars, the weather, lightning, the flight of birds, the livers and intestines of sacrificial animals, and dreams. A privileged caste of priests interpreted these omens and conveyed the will of the gods to the people. The Etruscans also had elaborate rituals connected with death; the body was cremated and the ashes buried in a special vase. The tomb was filled with important objects and decorated with scenes from daily life, including hunting, feasts, and domestic activities. The

Necropolis

The Etruscans devoted much attention to their burial ceremonies, which became more and more elaborate over the centuries. The first simple vase for the remains of the dead gave way to the sarcophagus, a coffin carved out of stone with inscriptions and scenes from daily life. Full-sized statues of the dead decorated the lids of many of these coffins.

The vase or sarcophagus was sometimes sealed in a cave but more commonly placed in a circular room dug into the ground. The domed roof of this room was covered with grass. This was the *tumulus*, or tomb. The domes of some of the largest tombs span over 150 feet (50 meters) in diameter.

Wishing to ease the passage of the dead to the afterlife, the Etruscans decorated the tombs with paintings depicting scenes from everyday life: hunting and fishing trips, games and athletic competitions, scenes from war—all activities tied to the life of the dead person. Buried alongside the dead were favorite objects and utensils. The *tumulus* began to look like a simple house.

Burial sites were placed only a short distance from Etruscan cities. As a cemetery grew, it became something of a village of its own, with a network of intersecting streets lined by many tombs. This was an Etruscan city of the dead, called a necropolis, found at every ancient Etruscan site.

Etruscans constructed entire cities of the dead. Indeed, most of what we know about daily life in Etruscan times comes, paradoxically, from their dead.

The decline of the Etruscan civilization began around 500 B.C. Attacked in the north by Celtic peoples, the Etruscans lost control over the Po River area within a hundred years. The Greeks battled the Etruscans in the south, defeating them around 450 B.C. The Italic tribes of Rome revolted against the Etruscans in 500 B.C., fighting for their independence and then for control over central Italy during the next one hundred years. The last major Etruscan town, Veio, fell to the Romans in 396 B.C. after ten years of battle. Over the next century, the Etruscans and their civilization were gradually absorbed by the rapidly expanding culture of Rome. By 250 B.C., the Etruscans had disappeared. Italy was now dominated by Rome.

But the influence of the Etruscans remained, even if their empire in Italy had disappeared. Just like the earlier foreigners—the Phoenicians and the Greeks—the Etruscans "lived on" in Roman Italy: Religion, politics, and society carried the traces of all these previous civilizations. The blending of so many different cultures, from the most ancient of the Italian peoples to the foreign civilizations of the Greeks and the Etruscans, has given modern Italy one of the Western world's most diverse and complex cultures.

Rome: Republic and Empire

The history of Rome is also the history of European civilization for nearly one thousand years. From its origins as a small village on the Tiber River, Rome expanded to dominate the central part of the Italian peninsula, and then spread its influence first through the entire Mediterranean, and then outward into Europe, North Africa, and the Middle East. A vast empire, its capital in the city of Rome, extended over the peoples of Europe (and some in Africa and Asia). Since its fall, this unity has not been seen again in Europe.

A marvelous legend recounts the foundation of the city of Rome. Twin brothers named Romulus and Remus, from an inland village, were abandoned by their mother, Silvia, who feared for their lives at the hands of a jealous king. Silvia placed the two tiny infants in a basket

The ruins of a temple stand at Ostia Antica, ancient Rome's port city on the Tiber River.   Magnum

and sent them down the Tiber River during a flood. The basket came to rest far downstream, caught in a tree as the waters subsided. Romulus and Remus were nearly dead of exposure and hunger. A female wolf found the two children and raised the boys as if they were her own cubs. Later, as young men, Romulus and Remus founded a new village at the site of their rescue by the wolf. The village was called Rome, named after Romulus, who won a competition with his brother.

In the low-lying land between two of Rome's hills, the Palatine and the Capitoline, Romulus set the foundations for a defensive wall to protect the new settlement. The construction of that wall marked the beginnings of Rome, and legend establishes the date as April 21, 753 B.C. (which is still celebrated as the birthday of Rome). But Remus refused to recognize the city named after his brother and leaped across the wall in defiance. Romulus killed his brother for this act.

Until very recently, modern historians considered the legend of Romulus and Remus to be a quaint myth, passed down from generation to generation over hundreds of years. But in the 1980's, archaeological excavations in the area between the Palatine and Capitoline hills lo-

---

"The Prize of Victory"

Rome fought Carthage in some of the bloodiest battles ever seen in human history during the Punic Wars, which lasted from 264 to 146 B.C. The Second Punic War, 218–201, was a milestone in history because Rome's victory gave the republic undisputed control of the Mediterranean.

However, Rome itself was almost destroyed in the midst of that war. The Carthaginian general Hannibal moved into Italy from Spain and France. He crossed the Alps at the head of an enormous army: 45,000 troops, 9,000 cavalry, and even 37 elephants. A courageous and daring general, Hannibal battled his way south and across the Apennines. In August 216 B.C., near the city of Cannae, Hannibal almost won the war. His cavalry outflanked the Roman army, killing nearly 50,000 soldiers.

Far from Carthage and without reinforcements, Hannibal could not attack the city of Rome directly. While he waited for more troops, Hannibal's position weakened. He was forced to abandon Italy and return to Carthage. The decisive moment came in 202 B.C. in North Africa. The Roman historian Livy describes the importance of this battle:

> Arrived in camp, Scipio [the Roman general] and Hannibal each urged their men to prepare both heart and hand for the

cated the remains of what appears to be the oldest wall in the city of Rome. It was found exactly where the legend said that Romulus constructed his wall. Sophisticated measurements of some fragments dated the wall's construction around 700 B.C. Science and archaeology apparently have confirmed some aspects of the centuries-old legend surrounding the foundation of Rome.

supreme struggle which, if Fortune smiled, would leave them victorious, not for a day only but for ever. Before the next night they would know whether Rome or Carthage was destined to give laws to the nations, for the prize of victory would be not Italy or Africa, but the whole world.

Next day, to decide this great issue, the two most famous generals and the two mightiest armies of the two wealthiest nations in the world advanced to battle, doomed either to crown or to destroy the many triumphs each had won in the past. In all hearts were mixed feelings, confidence alternating with fear. As men surveyed their own and the enemy's ranks, weighing the strength of each merely by what their eyes could tell them, thoughts of joy and of foreboding jostled for pre-eminence in their minds.*

Hannibal lost this epic battle. Much later, long after Hannibal's death, the Romans attacked Carthage and destroyed the city in 146 B.C. at the conclusion of the Third Punic War.

*From: Livy, *The War With Hannibal*, Books XXI–XXX of *The History of Rome From Its Foundation*, translated by Aubrey de Selincourt (New York: Penguin Books, 1981), pp. 658–659.

Lost in the past, the full story of the beginnings of Rome will probably never be known. Most likely founded around 850 B.C. by a Latin tribe that moved down out of the inland mountains to the valley of the Tiber River, Rome was a series of tiny settlements on seven hills. By 500 B.C., the small village had grown into a considerable city of several thousand people. The original wall had been extended to enclose the hills; a port, Ostia, had been built at the mouth of the Tiber; and other neighboring tribes had been incorporated into the area controlled by Rome.

The Roman Republic

All this had taken place under the rule of several kings who had brought the industry and skills of the Etruscans southward to the village on the Tiber River. Rome began to threaten other settlements in central Italy, which joined together to declare war on their growing rival. At the same time, a revolt within Rome by people who resented the powers of the king broke out. The last king, Tarquinius the Proud, was defeated, and the monarchy fell in 510 B.C.

Rome then became a republic, governed by two leaders called consuls. The citizens of Rome, free men from the city's most important families, elected the consuls. This was the beginning of representative government in Rome, even though only a select few could vote. There were three different representative bodies in the Republic: the Senate (which eventually had six hundred members); a council of ministers, judges, and administrators; and various assemblies of the many families of the city (the most important was a council of soldiers).

Over the next two hundred years, the common people of Rome gained political rights as well. They established their own council (but only after a threatened revolution in 494 B.C.) and a military assembly,

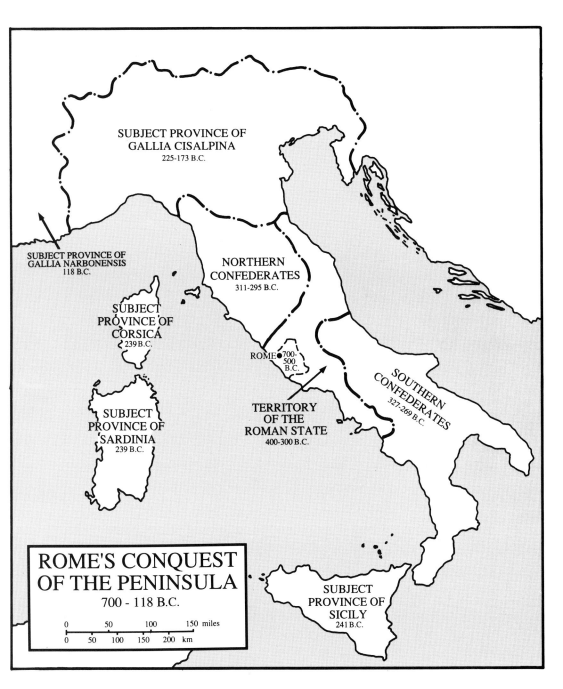

SUBJECT PROVINCE OF
GALLIA CISALPINA
225-173 B.C.

SUBJECT PROVINCE OF
GALLIA NARBONENSIS
118 B.C.

NORTHERN
CONFEDERATES
311-295 B.C.

SUBJECT
PROVINCE OF
CORSICA
239 B.C.

ROME ● 700-
500
B.C.

SUBJECT
PROVINCE OF
SARDINIA
239 B.C.

TERRITORY
OF THE
ROMAN STATE
400-300 B.C.

SOUTHERN
CONFEDERATES
327-269 B.C.

ROME'S CONQUEST
OF THE PENINSULA
700 - 118 B.C.

| 0 | 50 | 100 | 150 miles |

| 0 | 50 | 100 | 150 | 200 km |

SUBJECT
PROVINCE OF
SICILY
241 B.C.

using these two institutions to make their voice heard in the affairs of the city. The Republic drew up a written legal code around 450 B.C. All citizens were now equal before the law. This principle, and the code of law that accompanied it, was one of Rome's greatest contributions to Western civilization. The Latin motto of the Republic of Rome was *Senatus Populusque Romanus* (the "Senate and People of Rome"), or simply abbreviated as SPQR.

Rome Expands

By 400 B.C., the Republic ruled over all of central Italy, the Campania region in the south, and north to the Apennine Mountains. Rome had fought for these new lands, defeating the native tribes in the area and conquering the last resistance of the Etruscans. With the Roman victory over the Greeks in southern Italy (270 B.C.), the Republic became the most important state on the entire peninsula.

The next target for expansion was Rome's major competitor in the Mediterranean, the empire ruled from the North African city of Carthage. It took many battles over the next hundred years, but the Romans conquered the city of Carthage in 146 B.C.

This victory marked the high point of the Republic. Rome controlled the entire Mediterranean, and the Romans traded along all of its shores. They introduced a single currency, stamping first copper and then silver coins, to make trade easier throughout their vast territories.

Rome was originally an agricultural society, and the foundations of its economy were the shepherd and the family farmer working a small plot of land. However, as the city grew, commerce and industry became more important. The Romans traded widely, traveling as far as India, Arabia, and eastern Africa and dealing in spices, gold, ivory, silk, and perfumes. Roman industry developed around textiles, terra-cotta vases, and metal works.

The Forum

The focus of Roman life was the open squares of the city. These were called the forums, and they were the places where the Romans gathered to shop, worship, and carry on civic affairs. The most important of these squares, the one at the site where the city was founded, is now known simply as the Roman Forum.

The Forum's many temples made it the center of religious life of the Republic. Two enormous buildings, called Basilicas, served to house the government. The Roman Senate had its own meeting place in another building, the Curia. Stores and offices filled the rest of the Roman Forum. Monumental arches, built to celebrate victories in war, surrounded the Forum. In the very center, on the Via Sacra (Holy Road), stood a golden milestone. All the roads of Rome began from this point, and the marker listed the distances to the many territories of the Republic.

Today, little is left of the original Forum, but one can still gain an idea of the glory of ancient Rome by wandering among the ruins. The Forum is one of the most popular places for tourists when they visit modern Rome.

New Names for Old Gods

Roman culture was a fusion of the many different traditions existing throughout the lands of the Republic. The Romans adopted the Greek gods (though they changed their names) as well as Greek religious myths, adding a cult of nature drawn from the earlier Etruscan religion. Roman philosophy expanded on earlier Greek traditions while Roman art incorporated the style and subjects of both the Greeks and the Etruscans.

Roman architecture continued the Greek tradition of building temples, but the Romans devoted much more attention to civic architecture. Having perfected the vault and the dome and invented concrete, the Romans built enormous enclosed public buildings, including sports arenas, government offices, and public baths. Most public buildings in Rome were covered with marble, giving the city a splendor famous throughout the ancient world.

Literature in ancient Rome rested on the works of earlier civilizations but developed characteristics of its own as well. The greatest Roman poet, Vergil (70–19 B.C.), wrote the *Aeneid*, a twelve-volume history of the foundation of the city, which gave Rome an epic poem of the same stature as the *Iliad* and *Odyssey* from ancient Greece. In his-

Women in Rome

Women in both the Roman Republic and the Roman Empire had no legal or political rights, and their status depended largely on their economic position and their marriage.

Upper-class women acquired importance through their husbands. They received a literary education. Some became poets, others priests, a few lawyers and even public speakers. Women figured in Roman politics, but because they could not vote, their influence on decisions was felt behind the scenes.

Because their contribution to the family was essential, working women in Rome had to take on a wide variety of tasks. They were weavers, dressmakers, midwives, and doctors. Along with others in their family, they ran restaurants, grocery stores, and other small shops.

All women in Rome were held in deep respect as mothers. Their contribution in raising the next generation of Romans was widely acknowledged.

The Bocca della Verita *("Mouth of Truth") in Rome is an ancient round stone disc with the face of a water god. Legend says that a person who tells lies while resting a hand in the mouth gets an unpleasant surprise: It bites!* ENIT, Roma

tory (with the works of Livy and Tacitus), satire (Juvenal), politics (Cicero), and literature (Horace), the ancient Romans established a rich cultural tradition for Western civilization.

Roman Virtues

The family was the foundation of Rome, and it taught a code of ethical values that held Roman society together. Roman citizens were raised to consider six qualities fundamental to themselves and their Republic: virtue, freedom, religious faith, loyalty, involvement in civic affairs, and glory. These qualities were important in both private and public life.

All Roads Lead to Rome

The lands of the Roman Republic were divided into four categories. Rome was a magnificent capital of nearly one million people. The city, along with the surrounding territory, formed the core of the Republic, whose residents were the only ones with the right to vote. The "municipalities" included the other cities of the Republic, whose people were citizens but who could not vote. The "federations" were cities allied with Rome, but not officially incorporated into the Republic. The colonies were the far-spread lands that Rome occupied with its army and that supplied most of the food for the Republic.

Rome's wealth was based on expansion. New lands offered expanded trade opportunities and more food, increasing the prosperity of the Republic. Since new lands were gained through war, Rome's status rested on the Republic's military. The Roman army was enormous, perhaps as many as one million soldiers. The troops were well trained, well led, and dedicated. They were citizens as well as soldiers, and they fought hard for their Republic. But the Romans also had a "secret weapon": the roads. These roads, the ancient versions of modern freeways, were masterpieces of engineering, with such solid foundations and sophisticated paving that some of them still exist, nearly two thousand years later. The Roman army moved swiftly from one battle to the next over this network of roads that had the city of Rome as its hub. The phrase "All roads lead to Rome" has its origins in this massive construction project carried out by the military. Once the wars of expansion ended, the roads served to hold the Republic together.

One of the ancient Roman roads, the Appia Antica, headed south from the capital to Naples and then passed near the provincial town of Pompeii. The grooves in the paving stones were worn by centuries of foot and cart traffic.   ENIT, Roma

War not only brought new lands and new wealth to Rome, it also brought slaves from the conquered territories into the Republic. As Rome expanded, tens of thousands of slaves from all over Europe, the Mediterranean, and the Middle East became the work force of the Republic. Slaves harvested Rome's food in the colonies, worked in the mines, and manned the oars in the Republic's navy. Slaves also did more and more of the work in the cities, becoming public servants, shopkeepers, teachers, and doctors. Slaves could be freed, and they often were, by their owners.

Bread and Circuses

Slave labor contributed enormously to the wealth of both the Republic and the Empire of Rome. But the institution of slavery also weakened Rome. Slavery led to the ruin of thousands of peasant farmers, whose crops could no longer compete with the cheaper food harvested by slaves on large estates in Italy. Many farmers lost their land and their livelihood. They drifted to the capital city. No longer the basis of the Roman economy, the farmers turned into a large population of unemployed and discontented people in the city of Rome.

The leaders of both the Republic and Empire tried to satisfy the urban unemployed with welfare projects and entertainment. These were the "bread and circuses" of ancient Rome. Food was distributed to the poor, and sports arenas were built to distract the unemployed masses from their problems.

The city's poor and unemployed were still allowed to vote. Politicians and army generals played to the crowd in order to hold on to power. The support of those without work in the city was fickle, and more and more resources had to be devoted to keeping the city dwellers quiet. However, their grievances were never resolved, and their presence in the capital remained a threat to the stability of Rome.

Crossing the Rubicon: The End of the Republic

The growth of Rome would prove to be the downfall of the Republic. War and expansion made the army the most important institution in the Republic. Only the generals could guarantee new conquests and new wealth. As a result, they soon became the most important people in the Republic. It was only a matter of time until one of these powerful generals seized political power.

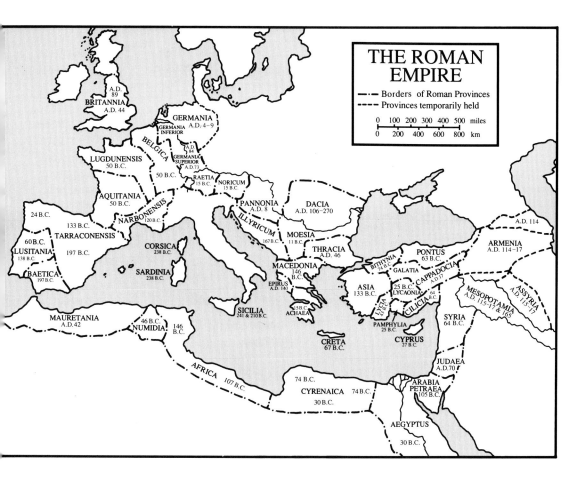

That man was Julius Caesar. Caesar was the military governor of France, and he conquered two other territories, England and Germany, between 55 and 53 B.C. He led an enormous army and enjoyed great popularity. The politicians in Rome feared that Caesar might try to take over the Republic. In 49 B.C., the Senators ordered him not to reenter Rome, but Caesar defied the Senate, crossed the northern boundary of the Republic at the Rubicon River, and returned to the capital city. He fought his political rivals, chasing one of them first to Greece and then all the way to Egypt (where Caesar met and fell in love with the Egyptian queen, Cleopatra).

Caesar then declared himself Emperor for Life. But his rule was a short one. Two political opponents, who objected to the title of Emperor, assassinated Caesar in March 44 B.C. A fortune-teller had warned Caesar that the "ides of March" (the fifteenth of the month) would be dangerous. The Emperor ignored those words, and ever since his murder, the "ides of March" have been synonymous with bad luck.

Other army generals followed Caesar, seizing political power for themselves. In 27 B.C., a new leader took the title of Augustus ("the highest"), and officially transformed the Roman Republic into an empire. For the next two hundred years, the Roman Empire enjoyed a monopoly on commerce and trade throughout the Mediterranean and Europe.

Augustus and the emperors who came after him spent much money in making Rome one of the most splendid cities in the world. The greatest monuments of Rome date from this period: an enormous sports stadium, the Colosseum (which had room for fifty thousand spectators); one of the world's biggest arenas, the Circus Maximus (with room for 100,000); grand theaters for plays; the public baths of Caracalla and Diocletian; and the great aqueducts built to supply Rome with water (the biggest was almost 50 miles, or 80 km., long).

United Europe

The Empire expanded ever farther into central Europe and the Middle East. Roman citizenship was extended to all the free male inhabitants of the Empire in A.D. 212, but it was the Emperor, not the people, who had the real political power. A single civilization, a single commercial market (now based on gold coins), a single government, and a common citizenship united the peoples of Europe and the Mediterranean.

However, signs of trouble appeared in the Empire at the height of its power. Political instability reigned in the capital of Rome as army generals fought for supremacy after A.D. 200. A period known as the years of "military anarchy," marked by frequent armed uprisings, lasted nearly seventy years. This weakened the Empire considerably.

Religious divisions also shook the Roman Empire. Augustus had been the first Roman emperor to insist that the citizens worship him as

Pompeii

South of Rome, near the city of Naples, stands a volcano, Mount Vesuvius. That volcano, which is still occasionally active, violently erupted on August 24, A.D. 79. The lava and cinder ash from Vesuvius buried the nearby Roman city of Pompeii. Virtually all of the twenty thousand inhabitants were killed. Out of this human tragedy came a historic windfall: a detailed look into the life of a provincial town at the height of the Roman Empire.

Preserved under the layers of lava and ash, Pompeii remains exactly as it was when the eruption began. Over the last two hundred years archaeologists have explored the ruins of the city. They have found a city with a central forum, a major aqueduct, temples, a theater and a sports arena, residential zones, and public baths. Pompeii was an agricultural trade center with many shops and markets. Items common in everyday life, such as household utensils, tools, and even bread, grains, and fruit were discovered.

Also buried under the eruption were the people of Pompeii, most of whom were unable to escape. Their bodies remained entombed in the lava. A visit to the ruins of Pompeii today provides the visitor with a rare glimpse into the past and an unforgettable encounter with a city doomed by a natural disaster nearly two thousand years ago.

All that remains of a giant statue of the Emperor Constantine are these pieces, now kept in the courtyard of the Capitoline Museum in Rome.   ENIT, Roma

a god. But a new religious group, the Christians, refused to recognize the divinity of the emperor. This threatened the basis of leadership in Rome. For two hundred years, the emperors struggled to dominate Christianity. Persecution and even the murder of several thousand Christians, however, failed. Emperor Constantine adopted the only solution left and granted the Christians religious freedom in A.D. 313. Several decades later, in 391, Christianity was made the Empire's official religion.

The very size of the Empire was another great problem. New people with different customs from faraway areas had been conquered as the empire had expanded. Integrating these peoples into Rome had become increasingly difficult. Frequent border wars plagued Rome and required a strong army, especially in the territories along the Danube River and in the Middle East.

The Fall of Rome

Rome had simply grown out of the control of its emperors. Italy was vulnerable to foreign attack, and the last of the great emperors, Constantine (who ruled from 312 to 337), moved the capital out of Rome. A new city, Constantinople (today called Istanbul, in Turkey), far away from the threatened Italian peninsula, became the capital. (See *The Land and People of Turkey.*)

The Empire was now divided between east and west. Over the next hundred years, the border wars grew more fierce. The city of Rome was first attacked in 410. The Huns, an eastern tribe from Siberia, fought the armies of the Empire, but the Romans defeated them in 451. The Vandals, a Germanic tribe, attacked and actually burned down the capital city of Rome in 455.

Another Germanic tribe, the Goths, also pushed at the fringes of the

Empire. The Romans chose not to fight the powerful Goths but to try to incorporate them. The Romans gave the Goths lands, first in the border areas and then more deeply within the Empire itself. The Romans admitted the Goths' soldiers into the Imperial armies, and some Goth leaders became provincial governors of Rome.

Within fifty years, the western Roman Empire simply disappeared, swallowed up by Germanic tribes on the peninsula. There was no final, decisive battle; rather, the Goths gradually absorbed the western Roman Empire and made it their own. One of the Goth leaders, Odoacre, took power from the last of the Roman emperors in 476.

The greatest civilization and largest empire that the European world has ever known fell apart. For the next three hundred years Italy was a peninsula occupied by and divided among several different non-Italian peoples, and the institutions and customs of Rome were gradually lost.

A part of Rome, however, continued to live on, but not in Italy. The eastern Roman Empire, called Byzantium, preserved Roman customs, art, literature, and law in the libraries and churches of Constantinople. Byzantium resisted the invasions of many German, Arab, and Asian peoples for almost a thousand years, but it could not defend itself against the Turks. They conquered Constantinople in 1453.

From Conquest to Rebirth: 500–1500

During the three hundred years following the fall of Rome, Italy became a battleground for the many different peoples of Europe. This series of conquests began with the invasion of the Lombards, who came into Italy from central Europe in the mid-500's. The Lombards defeated the Goths and Vandals, ruling over the northern areas of Italy and central Tuscany by 600. Moving southward, they consolidated their new conquests into the Lombard Kingdom of Italy.

The Lombard invasion threatened the Catholic Church in Italy as well. Christianity had grown in size and influence since its establishment as the official religion of the Empire. The Christians had established the formal Catholic Church and made Rome their capital city. They chose their own leader, called the Pope.

The Lombards' takeover of northern and central Italy worried the

Pope, who feared for his own safety and for the future of the Catholic Church. Looking for protection, the Pope invited the Franks, a Catholic people from the northwest (now France), into Italy to help defend the Church against the Lombards.

The Holy Roman Empire

The greatest of the Franks was Charlemagne, who waged war on the Lombards and defeated the last of them in 774. Charlemagne added northern and central Italy to his kingdom, which then extended throughout almost all of western Europe. In recognition of Charlemagne's conquests, the Pope crowned him as the leader of the new Holy Roman Empire on Christmas day, 800. Charlemagne had brought unity to the north and center of Italy for the first time since the fall of Rome. A period now known as the Middle Ages began. (See *The Land and People of France.*)

Charlemagne's unity did not last for long. The fight over who would become the new king after Charlemagne's death (in 814) weakened the empire. Over the next three hundred years, through 1100, central authority broke down, as many leaders claimed rights to the throne and the Holy Roman Empire.

Southern Italy was also changing. In 630, the Arabs began a holy war to establish an Islamic empire throughout the Middle East. In only a hundred years, they conquered Egypt and North Africa and invaded both Spain and southern France. In 827, the Arabs attacked Sicily. They made Palermo their capital city on the island, and for the next two hundred years, Sicily was part of the Islamic Empire.

Southern Italy soon saw more war. The Normans, originally from Scandinavia, arrived in the south around the year 1000. They fought first the Lombards and then the Arabs for control of southern Italy and Sicily from 1035 to 1092.

The People of Sicily

One of the recurrent themes in the history of Italy is the large number of peoples who came to live on the peninsula. Italian culture is the result of an extraordinary blend of the civilizations of all these people. Nowhere is this more true than the island of Sicily, whose history of foreign invasion and occupation dates back nearly three thousand years.

The native tribes of the island, the Sicles, were the first prehistoric peoples. In ancient times, first the Phoenicians (from Carthage in 800 B.C.), then the Greeks (beginning around 600 B.C.), and finally the Romans (who made Sicily their first colony around 240 B.C.) all ruled over the island. After the fall of the Rome, Sicily remained a part of the Byzantine Empire until the 800's when the Arabs arrived and occupied the island for the next two hundred years, from 827 to 1035. The Normans were the first western Europeans to rule Sicily, and they remained until 1189. Then came the Germans (through the 1200's). The French and Spanish fought for Sicily for over two centuries, with first the Spanish and then the French in control. Spanish rule came again and lasted from 1550 to 1714. The Austrians governed for a short period, followed by the Bourbons, who ruled from Naples. The island was one half of the Bourbons' Kingdom of the Two Sicilies from 1815 to 1860. Sicily became part of the Kingdom of Italy in 1861.

Feudal Society

The Franks and the Normans brought an important development to Italy: feudalism. Feudalism is the name given to the form of European society during the Middle Ages (from 800 to 1400). Feudal society was structured as a sort of pyramid. At the top stood the king, who

Church and State in the Middle Ages

Because Rome is the capital city of the Catholic Church, Italy has been at the center of disputes between politicians and the popes throughout the centuries.

One of the most important political issues in the Middle Ages was the question of who was the supreme ruler in Europe: the Pope or the Holy Roman Emperor. For over fifty years, from 1070 to 1122, the conflict focused on the power to choose the bishops of the Church.

Pope Gregory VII believed this was an issue best left to the Church. The Holy Roman Emperor, Henry IV, disagreed, believing that the king should make all decisions in his land. Henry deposed the Pope in order to make his point clear. The Pope responded by expelling the king from the Church.

Excommunication caused Henry IV serious problems. The Pope's action freed the lesser nobles from loyalty to the king by breaking the bond of religion that helped hold the feudal pyramid together. The first signs of revolt appeared. In order to preserve his throne, Henry was forced to seek the Pope's pardon. Gregory kept Henry waiting for three days in the cold and snow outside of a castle in Canossa (in the Italian Apennines) before receiving the king and readmitting him into the Church.

This hardly ended the dispute. After beating back the rebellious nobles, Henry again deposed the Pope in 1080. Gregory reacted by excommunicating Henry a second time. The seesaw battle for supremacy between church and state continued under Henry's son and two later popes. The issue was resolved only in 1122, when the Concordat of Worms established the supremacy of the Church in Italy. This decision gave the pope the power to appoint bishops. The Church's authority figured importantly in Italy well into the twentieth century.

commanded the loyalty of those below him. Underneath the king in the feudal pyramid stood a large number of nobles with various titles: lords, dukes, barons, counts, princes. Each of these men controlled his own land within the kingdom, and each pledged allegiance to the king. While women could rule these lands—as queens, countesses, etc.—it was almost always men who were in charge. The nobles lived off the food produced on their lands and the taxes they placed on the people. The nobles also had their own soldiers, called knights, and their armies banded together in case of invasion or rebellion.

Finally, on the lowest level of the feudal pyramid, stood the peasants: hundreds of thousands of men and women who worked on the lands of the royal nobles. The peasants lived in small rural villages. They were poor and their lives were extremely difficult. Agriculture was quite primitive in the Middle Ages, and survival was about the best the peasants could manage.

The collapse of the Roman Empire and the wars that followed for four hundred years put an end to widespread trade and industry. Rather, feudal society was based on agriculture. Land and food were the primary forms of wealth. Cities, once they were conquered, ceased to be the focus of civilization.

The Catholic Church was one of the key institutions in the feudal society of Italy. The Church owned its own land, made its own laws, and ruled over its own peasants. The pope in Rome was both a spiritual leader, the head of the Church, and something like an emperor himself, alongside the king.

The extent of the pope's power was clearly shown in a series of wars between 1096 and 1270. Several different popes ordered the nobles and kings of Italy and the rest of Europe to fight for the Catholic Church in the Holy Lands, the Middle East. These wars were called the Crusades, and no king dared to disobey the pope, even if many of the Crusades were disasters.

Francis of Assisi

Not everyone in Italy approved of the pope's power. Some Catholics believed that the Church should concern itself with religion and stay out of politics and war. The most famous of these dissenters was a young monk named Francis (1182–1226), who led a reform movement to return Christianity to its original, spiritual mission. Francis formed his own religious community and his movement attracted a wide following.

He was the son of a wealthy cloth merchant from the town of Assisi, in the foothills of Umbria. In his early twenties, Francis had a series of dreams or visions. He gave up a privileged life of luxury with his family and dedicated himself to prayer and to the service of God.

Four ideals guided the lives and work of Francis and his followers: humility, simplicity, poverty, and prayer. Francis's compassion extended to all animals, which he revered as creatures of God. His movement—called the Friars Minor—spread rapidly. By the end of the century, there were five hundred communities in Italy and several hundred more throughout Europe.

The Pope formally recognized the religious movement in 1223, three years before the death of Francis. Strict regulations governed the Franciscan friars. The rules of the community reveal the ideals and style of life of the Friars Minor:

If anyone wants to profess our Rule and comes to the friars . . . they should go and sell all that belongs to them and endeavor to give it to the poor. The friars may have one tunic with a hood and those who wish may have another without a hood. Those who are forced by necessity may wear shoes. All the friars are to wear poor clothes and they can use pieces of sackcloth and other material to mend them, with God's blessing.

When they travel about the world, they should not be quarrelsome or take part in disputes with words or criticize others; but they should be gentle, peaceful, and unassuming, courteous and humble, speaking respectfully to everyone, as is expected of them. They are forbidden to ride on horseback unless they are forced to it by manifest necessity or sickness. . . .

The friars . . . [may not] accept money in any form, either personally or through an intermediary. . . . The friars to whom God has given the grace of working should work in a spirit of faith and devotion and avoid idleness, which is the enemy of the soul, without however extinguishing the spirit of prayer and devotion, to which every temporal consideration must be subordinate. As wages for their labour they may accept anything necessary for their temporal needs, for themselves or their brethren, except money in any form. And they should accept it humbly as is expected of those who serve God and strive after the highest poverty.

The friars are to appropriate nothing for themselves, neither a house, nor a place, nor anything else. As strangers and pilgrims in this world, who serve God in poverty and humility, they should beg alms trustingly. And there is no reason why they should be ashamed, because God made himself poor for us in this world. This is the pinnacle of the most exalted poverty, and it is this, my dearest brothers, that has made you heirs and kings of the kingdom of heaven, poor in temporal things, but rich in virtue. This should be your portion, because it leads to the land of the living. And to this poverty, my beloved brothers, you must cling with all your heart, and wish never to have anything else under heaven, for the sake of our Lord Jesus Christ.*

Francis was made a saint of the Catholic Church in 1228. A major church was built in Assisi to house the Franciscan order, and Catholics today continue to revere Francis for his messages of simplicity and charity.

*From: Julius Kirshner and Karl F. Morrison (editors), *Readings in Western Civilization*, Vol. 4: *Medieval Europe.* (Chicago: University of Chicago Press, 1986), pp. 282–284.

Decline of Feudalism

Feudal nobles and the Church appeared to be at the height of their powers at the end of the Crusades. But behind the scenes, an important new development was taking place that would change the face of feudal Italy: the rise of cities.

Italian cities had never really disappeared during the five hundred years of invasion and settlement that followed the fall of Rome. However, their size and influence had certainly declined. Around the year 1000, the cities in Italy began to grow again as a result of the revival of international trade. The end of Arab expansion and the decline of the Byzantine Empire in Constantinople permitted Italy once again to assume the natural role geography had given it as the hub of Mediterranean trade.

The Maritime Republics

The first Italian cities to grow were those connected to commerce in the Mediterranean. These cities were called the Maritime Republics, because their economies were tied to travel on the seas and because they were ruled by representatives of the wealthiest merchant families. One of these cities was Amalfi, located on the western coast of Italy, south of Naples. Amalfi's fleet defeated an Arab navy in 849, and from that moment, the city dominated trade along the Tyrrhenian coast until the 1100's. A second Maritime Republic was Pisa. Pisa followed Amalfi as the major city on the Tyrrhenian Sea for the next two hundred years. Genoa, on the northern Ligurian Sea, was a third important trading city until the early 1400's.

The greatest of the Maritime Republics was Venice, which used its position at the head of the Adriatic Sea to act as the broker for goods

On the first Sunday of September, the gondolas of Venice take to the canals to celebrate the greatness of the Mediterranean trading empire that once belonged to this city. ENIT, Roma

moving between the Mediterranean and central Europe on the other side of the Alps.

Growth of Venice

The origins of the city of Venice lie in the 400's, when the Germanic invasion of northern Italy forced the local inhabitants off the mainland and out onto the islands of the nearby lagoon for their own survival.

Having defended themselves successfully, the Venetians expanded their holdings over the next four hundred years. By the end of the 900's, Venice controlled all of the northern and central Adriatic Sea.

Business in Genoa

Modern business practices began with the revival of trade in the eleventh century. The following contract, signed in 1086, establishes the responsibilities of two business partners—a financier and a commercial trader—in the Republic of Genoa. The letter also reveals the vast extent of the Genoan trade market.

I, Alberto Ceclieto, have received . . . from you, Bellobruno of Castello, one hundred sterling in Genoese money, which I shall take to Alexandria [Egypt] for the purpose of trading, and from there, should I wish, to Ceuta [Morocco] and I am to return to Genoa without any other change in my route. I am to send either to you or your designated agent the capital and the profit from this venture, and after the capital has been deducted, I am to keep one quarter of the profit.

I swear on the Holy Gospels to keep safe, watch over, and increase the investment . . . and to turn over and give to you or to your designated representative the capital and profit of the venture in good faith and with no deceit; and furthermore not to spend more than two shillings for expenses during the whole voyage.

Done at Genoa in the castle, at the house of Bellobruno, in the year 1086, . . . and the ninth day before the end of September . . . Ogerio Aragano and Ogerio Aguzzino, witnesses.*

*From: Thomas C. Mendenhall and Basil D. Henning (editors), *Ideas and Institutions in European History, 800–1715* (New York: Holt, Rinehart and Winston, 1964), pp. 93–95.

Soon afterward, the Venetians defeated the Normans and controlled the southern Adriatic as well. The religious wars of the Catholic Church helped expand Venice's territory further. In 1204, at the beginning of the Fourth Crusade, Venetians provided the Church's armies with ships to reach the Holy Land. In exchange, the Crusaders destroyed Zara (on the east coast of the Adriatic Sea), Venice's principal competitor, and occupied Constantinople.

By 1300, Venice was one of the most important and elegant international cities of the world, controlling the entire central and eastern Mediterranean. The population stood at nearly 100,000 people (more than that of Venice today). The wealthy families of merchants governed through their own councils, and they elected a single man, the doge, to administer the affairs of their empire.

The city's influence grew as its trade expanded. Venice's trade empire reached south to Greece and North Africa, and eastward into Syria and Persia. Always interested in expanding trade, the Venetians began to explore the Far East as well. Marco Polo, the most famous of the city's explorers, traveled as far as China between 1271 and 1295.

The Maritime Republics, and particularly Venice, were the first Italian cities to prosper from the revival of commercial trading. Trade soon sparked growth in many other Italian cities as well. In the fourteenth century, most of Europe's largest cities were in Italy: Milan, Florence, Naples, and Palermo each had more than fifty thousand inhabitants, as many as Paris. Even Bologna and Rome had forty thousand people, larger than London at the same time.

The Italian Cities

Italian cities dominated the revival of Mediterranean trade not only because of their geographic position but also because they produced high-quality, specialized products. Milan became a world leader in

Black Death

The gradual expansion of cities in Italy (and elsewhere in Europe) from 1100 to 1500 was marked by one major setback: the Black Death, or the Plague. The underlying disease, the bubonic plague, was a bacterial infection carried by fleas. When passed on to humans, the infection most often resulted in death.

The Plague began in Mongolia, in central Asia. It spread as the infected fleas, and the rats that carried them, moved along the trade routes that connected the Far East to Europe. The Black Death traveled by both land and sea out of China, around southeast Asia and India, up through the Persian Gulf to Turkey and finally out into the Mediterranean.

The Black Death reached Sicily toward the end of 1347. It spread quickly northward. From the ports of Genoa and Venice, the Plague reached the rest of Italy and most of France by the following summer. By June 1349, the Black Death was in England, and a year later it arrived in the countries of Scandinavia.

Doctors had no idea of what the disease was nor how to cure it. Hundreds of thousands died. Estimates of the loss of life from the Black Death range from 25 percent to 45 percent of the entire European population.

The Plague struck with particular ferocity in European cities. Florence was one of the first inland cities in Italy to suffer. Boccaccio, a writer living in the city at time, guessed that over 100,000 people died. He described the disease in his masterpiece *The Decameron*:

> Its earliest symptom, in men and women alike, was the appearance of certain swellings in the groin or the armpit, some of

which were egg-shaped whilst others were roughly the size of a common apple. Sometimes the swellings were large, sometimes not so large, and they were referred to by the populace as plague boils. . . . [The] deadly boil would begin to spread, and within a short time it would appear at random all over the body. Later on, the symptoms of the disease changed, and many people began to find dark blotches and bruises on their arms, thighs and other parts of the body, sometimes large and few in number, at other times tiny and closely spaced. These, to anyone unfortunate enough to contract them, were just as infallible a sign that he would die as the boil had been earlier . . .

[Few] of those who caught it ever recovered, and in most cases death occurred within three days from the appearance of the symptoms described, some people dying more rapidly than others, the majority without fever or other complications.

But what made this pestilence even more severe was that whenever those suffering from it mixed with people who were still unaffected, it would rush upon these with the speed of a fire. . . . Nor was this the full extent of its evil, for not only did it infect healthy persons who conversed or had any dealings with the sick, making them ill or visiting an equally horrible death upon them, but it also seemed to transfer the sickness to anyone touching the clothes or other objects which had been handled or used by its victims.*

*From: Giovanni Boccaccio, *The Decameron.* (New York: Penguin Books, 1984), pp. 50–51.

Lucca and the Silk Industry

Perhaps the best example of specialization was the small Tuscan city of Lucca. This city built its wealth on a luxury good, silk. The creation of a silk industry in the late Middle Ages was nothing short of miraculous. The silkworms originally came from China and had been introduced to Italy by the Arabs in Sicily. The silkworms ate the leaves of mulberry trees and spun their cocoons with a fine thread that was processed into silk cloth. It took nearly one ton (.9 metric ton) of mulberry leaves for the silkworms to produce only twelve pounds (5.45 kilograms) of raw silk.

The demand for silk was strong in Europe and the profits were high. More and more land was planted with mulberries. In the 1330's and 1340's, eight thousand tons of mulberry leaves were fed to the silkworms, so that Lucca could produce 100,000 pounds (45,000 kilograms) of raw silk each year.

wool. The region of Lombardy developed a cotton industry second to none. The city of Florence concentrated on textile and leather goods. Other cities developed different specialities.

Banking Trade also required money and financing, and again Italian cities led the way. The gold coins of Florence (the *fiorino*) and Venice (the *ducato*) were honored throughout Europe. Some merchants began to deal exclusively in money, investment, and exchange. In the Tuscan city of Siena, the Bank of the Monte dei Paschi became one of the world's most important financial institutions. The wealthy bankers of Siena influenced not only the marketplace but also the political affairs of the cities and even those of the Catholic Church.

Medieval towers in the city of Bologna. Important families built towers as a sign of their wealth and status, but they also served for defense during the civil wars common in the cities during the Middle Ages. ENIT, Roma

The Lamentation, *painted by Giotto in 1306, depicts the suffering of Mary at the death of Jesus. This fresco is one of a series in the Arena Chapel in Padua.* Syracuse University, Florence

The expansion of trade brought prosperity and growth to the cities. This new wealth, however, lay outside the boundaries of feudal society and its economy based on land and agriculture. Though both the nobles and the Church hoped to control the towns and their new-found wealth, the Italian cities managed to play the Church off against feudal nobles throughout the 1200's and 1300's, eventually gaining independence from both. This marked the beginnings of the Italian city-state.

By the 1300's, there were about a dozen city-states in Italy, including Milan, Padua, Venice, Lucca, Pisa, Siena, Florence, and Perugia. Each of these cities dominated the surrounding area. Government was carried out by a representative council of nobles and townspeople who rarely agreed on civic affairs.

Florence, with 100,000 people, was one of the largest of these inde-

pendent city-states. Florence had been an important town for textiles (cotton and wool) from Etruscan times. The city continued to
prosper during both the Roman Republic and Empire. Located on the
Arno River, as far upstream as boats could sail from the Tyrrhenian
coast, Florence had become a major inland port by the 1100's. One
hundred years later, Florence imported raw wool from England, processed the wool, and then sold it throughout Europe. Six thousand people worked in Florence's textile industry. The Florentine merchants
grew rich over the years, and they gradually dominated the poorer nobles whose wealth came from land, not trade and industry. The city extended its control into new areas of Tuscany, conquering Siena, Arezzo,
and Pisa.

Rival factions fought for power in Florence and in other city-states.
Bloody battles among feudal landlords, representatives of the Church,
and the town merchants lasted for nearly two hundred years. In
Florence, Italy's greatest poet, Dante Alighieri, found himself on the
losing side in one of these wars and was exiled from the city in 1302.

By the mid-1300's, it was clear to the merchants of Florence that
such wars only hurt business. They demanded a new government for
Florence, no longer made up of representatives of either the Church or
the nobility, but rather an assembly of the merchants themselves. Eight
men chosen by this new assembly served as an elected administrative
council of Florence called the *Signoria*. Variations on the *Signoria*—
sometimes with only one leader—appeared in most of the other Italian
city-states at about the same time. The towns could now get on with
the business of trade and industry. The rule of the wealthy families had
begun.

The most important family in Florence was the Medici, who served
as the bankers for the city and its merchants. Florence prospered under the influence of the Medici and the rule of the businessmen.
Wealthy Florence became the focus of the rejuvenation of European
culture, nine hundred years after the fall of the Roman Empire.

Dante and The Divine Comedy

Dante Alighieri (1265–1321) was Italy's greatest poet, and one of the foremost literary geniuses of Western civilization. In the three books of his masterpiece, *The Divine Comedy*, Dante offers a vivid portrayal of the medieval world and the major philosophical and religious issues of his time. *The Divine Comedy* was the first major work written in Italian, rather than Latin, and opened the way for the development of Italian literature. The poem also established the Tuscan version of Italian as the standard form of the Italian language.

Dante wrote *The Divine Comedy* in 1312, a decade after his exile from Florence. The poem is the story of the author's tour of the Inferno (Hell), Purgatory, and Paradise. It also contains sharp criticisms of the rulers and nobles of Italy (including the Pope) for the destruction they had brought to Dante's native city. But perhaps most memorable are his descriptions of Hell:

> *I am in the third circle, in the round of rain*
> *eternal, cursed, cold and falling heavy,*
> *unchanging beat, unchanging quality.*
> *Thick hail and dirty water mixed with snow*
> *come down in torrents through the murky air,*
> *and the earth is stinking from this soaking rain.*
> *Cerberus, a ruthless and fantastic beast,*
> *with all three throats howls out his doglike sounds*
> *above the frowning sinners of this place.*

His eyes are red, his beard is slobbered black,
   his belly swollen, and he has claws for hands;
   he rips the spirits, flays and mangles them.
Under the rain they howl like dogs, lying
   now on one side with the other as a screen,
   now on the other turning, these wretched sinners.
When the slimy Cerberus caught sight of us,
   he opened up his mouths and showed his fangs;
   his body was one mass of twitching muscles.
My master stooped and, spreading wide his fingers,
   he grabbed up heaping fistfuls of the mud
   and flung it down into those greedy gullets.
As a howling cur, hungering to get fed,
   quiets down with the first mouthful of his food,
   busy with eating, wrestling with that alone,
So it was with all three filthy heads
   of the demon Cerberus, used to barking thunder
   on these dead souls who wished that they were deaf.*

*From: Dante Alighieri. *The Divine Comedy*, Volume 1: *Inferno*, translated by Mark Musa. (New York: Penguin Books, 1984), pp. 121–122.

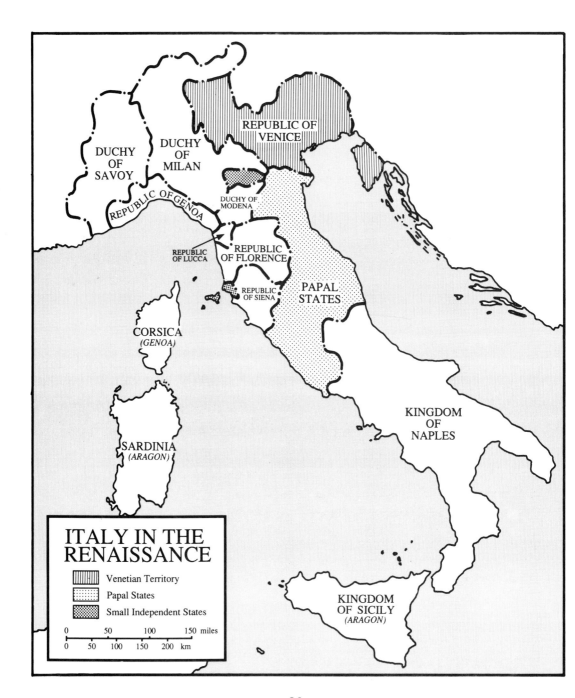

ITALY IN THE RENAISSANCE

Venetian Territory
Papal States
Small Independent States

REPUBLIC OF VENICE

DUCHY OF SAVOY

DUCHY OF MILAN

REPUBLIC OF GENOA

DUCHY OF MODENA

REPUBLIC OF LUCCA

REPUBLIC OF FLORENCE

REPUBLIC OF SIENA

PAPAL STATES

CORSICA
(GENOA)

SARDINIA
(ARAGON)

KINGDOM OF NAPLES

KINGDOM OF SICILY
(ARAGON)

0   50   100   150 miles
0   50 100   150   200 km

The Renaissance

The period from 1400 to 1550 is called the Renaissance (in Italian, the *Rinascimento*), a word meaning "rebirth." Greek and Roman literature, science, art, and philosophy were "reborn" and used during the Renaissance to develop a new European culture.

Renaissance thinkers rejected the medieval understanding of the world based on religion and superstition and on the importance of destiny and luck in human affairs. Instead, the Renaissance outlook stressed the active and creative role of people as they explored and improved the world around them. "Humanism" was the term given to this concept.

During the Renaissance, many Italian cities, now politically independent and wealthy, eagerly accepted the humanist outlook. Citizens and rulers alike looked for a new philosophy to guide their new age. The wealthy cities of Renaissance Italy could also afford to support scholars and artists in their work. Italy experienced a cultural explosion as ancient values blended with the secular spirit of a money-making age. This was particularly true in Florence, one of the most important Italian city-states.

The classic texts of Greece and Rome served as the foundations for Renaissance humanism. These works were known throughout the Middle Ages, but their influence had remained limited, confined to monasteries and available in only a few editions, each copied by hand. What was new during the Renaissance was the spread of this earlier knowledge throughout Italy and northern Europe among a growing literate population in the cities.

The fullest understanding of Greek and Roman works required a profound knowledge of the two civilizations. In Italy, Petrarch (1304–1374) was an early advocate of this approach. Those who fol-

The Sacrifice of Isaac, *sculpted by the artist Ghiberti in 1402–1403, won first prize in a competition to decorate the doors of the baptistry in Florence's main square. It is now in the city's Bargello Museum.*   Syracuse University, Florence

The Printing Press

The Renaissance became so important in Western civilization because it spread from Italian city-states throughout Europe. The invention of the printing press made this possible. The Chinese had developed the first techniques of printing, and the Arabs had perfected the art of papermaking. Both skills arrived in Italy, following the trade routes from Asia and Africa to Europe. The German printer Johannes Gutenberg was the first to perfect a modern printing press using movable type, an invention of far-reaching consequences, in the mid-1400's. By 1467, the technology had come to Italy, and Italian publishers took the lead in the production of scholarly manuscripts.

The printing press was a revolution in communications. Multiple copies of a single work could be easily produced and distributed among large numbers of people. This simultaneously created and satisfied a growing reading public. Literate Europeans began to share a common body of knowledge and a cultural network formed among authors, teachers, publishers, and political leaders. Only the Phoenicians' development of a written alphabet made a greater contribution than the printing press to Western culture and knowledge.

lowed Petrarch formed their own schools for the study of classical literature, philosophy, and history. These scholars gathered together, summarized, and taught the lessons of the past.

Building on the traditions of the past, Renaissance thinkers advanced their understanding of the world. Mathematics was an important field of study. New studies of arithmetic, geometry, and algebra during the Renaissance formed the basis of modern science. Liberated from the rigid dogmas of religion, backed up by mathematics and sponsored by merchants interested in understanding the real world, Italians rediscovered the rigors of scientific investigation and the experimental method. The great Renaissance figures in this field were Leonardo da Vinci (1452–1519), who was not only a scientist but also an inventor, artist, and designer, and Galileo Galilei (1564–1642), mathematician, astronomer, scientist, physicist, and inventor.

From the study of mathematics came new discoveries about proportion and perspective. These ideas influenced Renaissance architecture. The mastery of proportions led to the construction of elegant and harmonious buildings. In Florence and in other Italian Renaissance cities, wealthy citizens sponsored building projects to beautify their towns and to show their wealth and status. Elaborate palaces and impressive town halls arose in Italian cities. Some of the greatest architectural masterpieces of the Renaissance are in Florence: the Bell Tower, by Giotto in 1400; the dome of the church Santa Maria dei Fiore, by Brunelleschi in 1434; the Palazzo Medici-Riccardi, by Michelozzo in 1440; Palazzo Strozzi, by Pollaiuolo in 1488; and the Laurentian Library, by Michelangelo in 1559.

The arts, in particular, were reborn during the Renaissance. Freed from the exclusive patronage of the Catholic Church, painting and sculpture rediscovered older ideals of beauty from classical times, and brought these up to date with new ideas and new techniques, utilizing discoveries of proportion and perspective. Much art still focused on stories from the Bible, but these new works had a grace and style that reflected a more secular spirit. The portraits by Botticelli (circa 1444–1510), the paintings by Titian (called Tiziano in Italian,

Michelangelo's statue of David, 1501–1504, is one of the masterpieces of Renaissance art. The David *demonstrates perfect technique and embodies the philosophy of its age: the pride, power, beauty, and nobility of humanity. Over 14 feet (4.25 meters) high, the statue now stands in the Accademia Museum in Florence.* Syracuse University, Florence

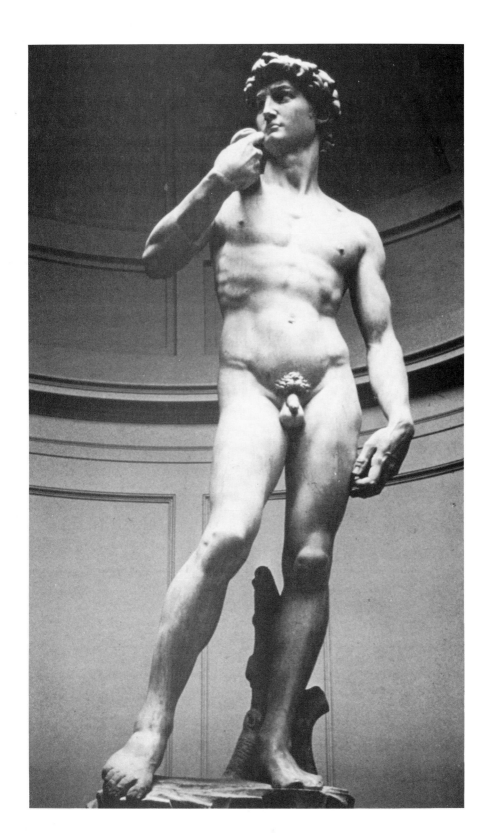

Michelangelo

Michelangelo Buonarroti (1475–1564) is often portrayed as the ideal "Renaissance man." He was not only one of the greatest sculptors of all time but was also famous for his architecture, paintings, and poetry. His mastery in so many areas made him the central figure in the art of the Renaissance.

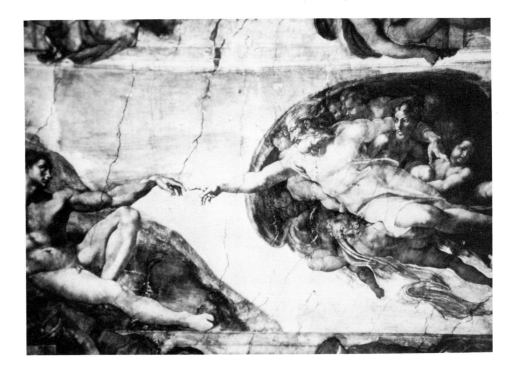

1477–1576), the frescoes of Raphael (in Italian, Raffaello, 1483–1520), and the sculptures of both Ghiberti (1378–1455) and Donatello (1386–1466) demonstrate the new spirit of the Renaissance. These artists, major figures in the Italian Renaissance, all worked in Florence

Michelangelo came from a small Tuscan town near Arezzo. He studied in Florence, where he found an important sponsor in the Medici family. His career took off from that point, and Michelangelo became the most sought-after artist of his day.

The list of works commissioned from Michelangelo is a long one. Michelangelo gave Florence the finest of all Renaissance sculptures—the *David*. Other important works in Florence included the tombs for the Medici family, the Laurentian Library, and the *Pietà* for the city's cathedral. Michelangelo also worked for the popes in Rome for many years. He painted the frescoes for the Sistine Chapel of the Vatican, he sculpted another *Pietà* and a *Moses* for the Pope, and he designed St. Peter's cupola and the main square in the Capitoline Hill.

The quality of Michelangelo's work is superb. At times even he was impressed by how much emotion some of his work conveys. The statue of Moses projects so much life and spirit that Michelangelo is rumored to have once asked his sculpture, *"Perche non parli?"* (Why don't you talk?).

Michelangelo painted scenes from the Bible to decorate the ceilings of the Sistine Chapel in Rome. One of the most famous panels is the Creation of Adam *(1511).* Syracuse University, Florence

at some point in their careers. Michelangelo, also a Florentine artist, created what many people consider the two greatest works of the Renaissance: the statue of David (on display in Florence) and the frescoes for the Sistine Chapel in Rome.

Machiavelli

Niccolò Machiavelli (1469–1527) was a statesman and diplomat at the height of Florence's power. He served the Florentine Republic for fifteen years, but he faced a charge of treason and was sentenced to prison when the government changed hands in 1512. The next year, hoping to gain favor with the new leaders, Machiavelli wrote *The Prince*, a guide to gaining and holding political power. Machiavelli, like other Renaissance figures, drew examples from ancient Rome (especially from the historian Livy) to illustrate his points. This passage from *The Prince* shows how Machiavelli studied questions of power directly, with few concessions to morals and sentiments:

> From this arises the following question whether it is better [for a Prince] to be loved than feared, or the reverse. The answer is that one would like to be both the one and the other; but because it is difficult to combine them, it is far better to be feared than loved if you cannot be both. One can make this generalization about men: they are ungrateful, fickle, liars, and deceivers, they shun danger and are greedy for profit; while you treat them well, they are yours. They would shed their blood for you, risk their property, their lives, their children, so long, as I said above, as danger is remote; but when you are in danger they turn against you. . . .

> The prince must nonetheless make himself feared in such a way that, if he is not loved, at least he escapes being hated. For fear is quite compatible with an absence of hatred. . . .

> So, on this question of being loved or feared, I conclude that since some men love as they please but fear when the prince pleases, a wise prince should rely on what he controls, not on what he cannot control. He must only endeavor, as I said, to escape being hated.*

*From: Niccolò Machiavelli, *The Prince*, translated by George Bull. (New York: Penguin Books, 1982), pp. 96–98.

The Florentine sculptor Donatello created his own David, *a much different treatment of the biblical story of the fight against the giant Goliath. Donatello's bronze statue, only 62 inches (158 centimeters) tall, is another masterpiece of the Italian Renaissance, dating from circa 1440. Bargello Museum, Florence.* ENIT, Roma

The Renaissance outlook encouraged both knowledge of the world and plans to improve it. The humanists took up an active role in society and civic life. The result was the development of modern politics. Drawing on examples from ancient Rome, Renaissance thinkers made politics a science, too. Italians taught the art of statecraft to many of Europe's rulers through the seventeenth century. Niccolò Machiavelli, from Florence, was the leading figure in Renaissance politics.

Voyages of Discovery

Curiosity about the world and interest in new trade routes also led to great voyages of exploration. Explorers sailed westward from Europe and came across North and South America, which they called the "New World." Many of these voyages were the undertakings of Italians, the most famous of whom was Christopher Columbus (in Italian, Cristoforo Colombo). Columbus, from Genoa, sailed for the king and queen of Spain to the Americas in 1492. John Cabot (originally Giovanni Caboto) came from Venice and sailed to North America and Canada in 1498 for the English. Amerigo Vespucci, a Florentine from whom came the name "America," explored for the Portuguese and reached South America in 1501. Giovanni Verrazzano, also a Florentine, charted the Atlantic coast of North America for the French.

These voyages of exploration not only opened up new trade routes but brought new and different products back to Europe. For Italy, one of the most important of these was the tomato (from South America), which later became a staple in the Italian diet.

The voyages were a sign of the power of the Renaissance, but they were also the downfall of the Italian cities. The discovery of the New World shifted trade away from Europe and toward the Americas. Commercial activity moved out of the Mediterranean Sea and into the

Atlantic Ocean. Countries like Spain, Portugal, France and England were in the best position to profit from the new trade possibilities with North and South America. Italy gradually ceased to be the center of international commerce, and the Italian city-states, too far away from these new markets, began to decline.

The Spanish brought back vast amounts of gold and silver from South America. Spain became the richest and most powerful nation in the world (see *The Land and People of Spain*). And when the Spaniards (as well as the French) invaded the Italian peninsula, the independent city-states of Italy found themselves no match for these great nations. The Spaniards occupied most of the south of the peninsula. The French defeated Florence. The other city-states in Italy, except for Venice, suffered similar fates. For the next two hundred years, Italy was divided into many small countries, each ruled by foreign powers.

Creating Italy: 1500–1870

Though the idea of a single, unified Italy goes back to Greek times, the modern nation of Italy formed little more than one hundred years ago. Before 1861, Italy was only a "geographic expression," a peninsula subdivided into many separate, smaller countries.

From the end of the Renaissance in the late 1500's, Italy was occupied by both the French and the Spanish. These two nations, newly powerful on the European continent, fought for control of the Italian peninsula in many wars. Government in some areas of Italy shifted back and forth between the two occupiers.

Sicily, for example, was first ruled by the French and then by the Spanish. France and Spain also fought for control of the land around Naples. French and Spanish kings battled over Milan, and for Lombardy, Tuscany, and Sardinia. For nearly forty years France and

Spain were in a permanent state of war in Italy. Finally, in 1559, the Spanish decisively beat the French. For the next 150 years, much of Italy was a Spanish colony.

Unending wars between foreign powers made an already difficult life that much harder for the peasant population of Italy. The triumph of Spain in the mid-1500's was an economic and social disaster for Italy, particularly in the south. The Spaniards' primary interest was to take as much wealth as possible. During the period of the Spanish domination, Italy was poorly administered and heavily taxed. Under the Spaniards, the Catholic Church reacquired the leading role in society temporarily lost during the Renaissance.

Spanish rule in Italy ended in war. Near the city of Turin in 1706 the armies of England, Austria-Hungary, Holland, and Savoy (a region in the northwest corner of Italy) defeated the Spanish and French forces. Peace came in 1714. Austria-Hungary, the victorious nation closest to Italy, acquired the greatest influence on most of the Italian peninsula for the next hundred years.

Twelve Italys

By this time there were really twelve different countries on the peninsula. Five of these were particularly important: the Kingdom of Sardinia, which included the northwestern area called Piedmont as well as the island of Sardinia; the Kingdom of Lombardy, the area around the city of Milan, whose rulers were tied to the king of the Austro-Hungarian Empire; the Grand Duchy of Tuscany, with its capital city, Florence; the Kingdom of Naples; and the Kingdom of Sicily. There were also three republics—Genoa, Lucca, and Venice—and three small duchies—Massa/Carrara, on the Tyrrhenian coast, and Parma and Modena, both in the region called Emilia. And finally, there were the Papal States, a federation of individual regions (in Emilia, the Marches,

Church and Science: Galileo Galilei

Galileo Galilei (1564–1642) was an outstanding physicist, scientist, and inventor in late-Renaissance Europe. He came from a Florentine family but was born in Pisa, where he studied mathematics and physics. In a famous demonstration, Galileo dropped objects of different weights from the Leaning Tower of Pisa. He noted that they all reached the ground at the same time. Based on these experiments, Galileo developed a modern theory of gravity.

In 1592, the Republic of Venice offered Galileo a high salary and a position at the University of Padua. There Galileo taught physics and geometry, expanding his studies into the field of astronomy.

Galileo's fame, and his trouble with the Catholic Church, began with the exploration of the night sky. He invented his own telescope, a much-improved version of the primitive ones already available, and began to manufacture and market them as navigational aids to traders in Venice.

Umbria, and Lazio) that were ruled by the pope in Rome.

Each of these twelve countries had a different leader: a king, a duke, or a papal representative. Each had its own government and laws. The people in most of these nations spoke their own language and had different money, taxes, habits, and customs. In the mid-1700's, there was really no such thing as "Italy," only twelve different countries, each with its own history and identity.

All that changed with the French Revolution in 1789. One of the new ideas associated with the French Revolution was that a nation is really made up of its *people*, not merely its king, nobles, or representatives of the Church. This idea is called nationalism, and it formed the

After lengthy observations, Galileo published two studies that amounted to a revolution in how people understood the universe: Galileo maintained that the Earth orbited around the sun and moved in the same way as other stars and planets.

The Pope, Urban VIII, objected to these conclusions. Denying that the Earth was the center of the universe and that instead it moved through the heavens, Galileo not only contradicted the teachings of the Church but also appeared to cast doubt on God's interest in human affairs. Galileo was brought before a Church court and convicted of heresy. Faced with the prospect of torture and imprisonment, Galileo denied his own discoveries—although he was later reported to have muttered, "*Eppur si muove* (It *does* move)." Modern science suffered a major setback at Galileo's trial. The dogmas of the Church temporarily beat back the Renaissance and humanist goal of a rational, scientific understanding of the world. (Toward the end of the twentieth century, the Church admitted its error in convicting Galileo.)

basis of modern ideas about democracy and the right to self-rule.

Many educated people in the towns of the twelve "Italys" were attracted to this new idea about the nation. They, like the revolutionaries in France who overthrew their king, wanted a voice in their own government. And in the larger Italian cities, such as Turin, Milan, Parma, Modena, Bologna, Florence, and Naples, people began to talk about change and about replacing the local rulers—kings, dukes, and even the pope—with elected representatives of the people.

But though this idea was strong, its advocates were weak and unable to stand up to the local rulers. Change became possible only when Napoleon Bonaparte, at the head of the army of the French Revolution, invaded the peninsula of Italy. Austria-Hungary was the greatest enemy of France in 1796, and Napoleon decided to fight the Austrians in northern Italy.

Napoleon in Italy

France's war against Austria-Hungary changed the face of Italy. Marching 45,000 soldiers across the snowy Alps in March 1796, Napoleon first defeated the troops of the Kingdom of Sardinia (in only twenty-five days) and then battled the Austro-Hungarians in Lombardy. Napoleon won that war early in 1797 and declared Milan the capital of a new country, the Cisalpine Republic. The French success in northern Italy set off great changes elsewhere on the peninsula. First, the Pope, in order to prevent Napoleon from marching on Rome, surrendered the northern Papal States of Bologna and Ferrara to the French. Then the people of Parma and Modena revolted against their Austro-Hungarian dukes and asked for Napoleon's protection. Parma and Modena joined the Cisalpine Republic. Napoleon lent his support to a revolt in Genoa and then annexed that republic to his new Cisalpine nation. The French also seized Lucca. All this took place in less than two years.

Napoleon Bonaparte returned to the peninsula in 1800, and over the next decade he finished redrawing the map of Italy. He first made the Cisalpine Republic a new Italian Republic (and appointed himself its president), then changed its title to the Kingdom of Italy (and appointed himself its king). He annexed the Piedmont area and all of the Grand Duchy of Tuscany to the French Empire. The French conquered Venice in 1805 and added it to the Kingdom of Italy as well. Napoleon installed his brother as the new king of Naples and, after conquering the city of Rome, declared the end of the pope's rule and took over the remaining Papal States.

Italy had been created by the French. Gone were the twelve countries of the mainland. In their place were only three: an extension of the French Empire onto the Italian peninsula, a new Kingdom of Italy in the north, and a French-governed Kingdom of Naples in the south. The only areas left untouched by the French were the islands of Sardinia and Sicily.

The effects of the French conquest were enormous and contradictory. Napoleon brought efficient administration to his Italian lands; he introduced a single currency and a common system of weights and measures; and he unified all law under one legal code. Napoleon also granted people in Italy the opportunity to govern their own local affairs, though their decisions were always subject to approval by the French authorities. The French leader gave the Italians their first experience of unity and limited self-government in several hundred years.

But the French occupation was also a harsh one. Taxes, a military draft, war, and death also marked French rule and created much resentment toward Napoleon and his army.

Reaction and Restoration

The unity that France brought to Italy lasted only as long as Napoleon. Austria-Hungary, England, Prussia (the forerunner to Germany), and Russia defeated the French in 1814 and 1815. The victorious countries then had to decide what to do with an Italy that had been dramatically changed by Napoleon. In 1815, at the Congress of Vienna, they decided to erase all signs of the French Revolution. Old rulers were put back on their thrones and Europe returned to its past.

The restoration of the kings and dukes in Italy meant a return to the division of the peninsula into many different countries. Eight nations were re-created in 1815: the Kingdom of Sardinia, with the former Republic of Genoa; the Kingdom of Lombardy, with Venice; the Grand

Duchy of Tuscany, with Lucca; the duchies of Massa/Carrara, Parma, and Modena; the Papal States; and the single Kingdom of the Two Sicilies, combining both Naples and Sicily. It was as if Napoleon had never existed. Austria-Hungary, the country with the closest ties to Italy, pledged to block all future change on the peninsula.

Risorgimento

A confusing period followed the Restoration. For the next forty-five years Italians in many different cities worked to introduce the beginnings of self-rule in their own areas. Time and again, cities rose up in revolution against their local rulers, only to see their demands for change crushed by the Austro-Hungarian military forces. This period (from 1815 to 1861) is called the *Risorgimento*, which in Italian means "reawakening" or "resurgence."

The dukes and kings in each of the many Italys refused to accept any form of political change. All activity that challenged these rulers was declared illegal. This forced those people interested in change to work secretly so as to avoid arrest, jail, exile, or even execution. In the Italy of the *Risorgimento* years, a great number of secret societies flourished and acted as the center for ideas and action.

Carbonari   Some of these secret societies had unusual names, such as the League of the Sublime and Perfect Masters. Others, such as the Masons, gathered together shopkeepers, students, and lawyers in Italy and throughout all of Europe. The most important of all the secret societies was the *Carbonari*, who took their name from the charcoal burners of the Italian hills. The *Carbonari* were active in most of the larger Italian towns, including Naples, Turin, Modena, Parma, and Genoa. They demanded limits on the absolute powers of the kings and dukes. The *Carbonari* wanted a constitutional monarchy, based on a written constitution that guaranteed political rights and a parliament for representative government. They also worked to gain the support of local army leaders, hoping to attract the military to their revolution.

The *Carbonari* (and other secret societies) led several uprisings in many cities on the Italian peninsula. In 1820, Naples and Turin rose up against their rulers and demanded a constitution and a representative government. In 1830, revolutions took place in Modena, Parma, and Genoa, and in towns of the Papal States in Emilia, the Marches, and Umbria. The people of the cities carried out revolutions that temporarily ended the power of the local rulers (including the representatives of the Pope). Some of these revolutions lasted only a few days, while others (in Modena, for example) lasted several months. Revolution in all of these areas, however, ended shortly after the deposed rulers called for Austro-Hungarian help. Troops sent from Vienna defeated each uprising, one after the other. The dukes, kings, and papal legates were restored to power by the Austro-Hungarian army.

Revolution in 1848

Revolution spread through all of Europe in 1848. In country after country, people in the cities rose up to demand democratic rights and representation. In Italy, revolution in 1848 began in Milan, the capital city of the Kingdom of Lombardy. For five days in mid-March the people of Milan rioted. The Austro-Hungarian army was unable to defeat the revolution. Milan declared its independence.

Revolution spread quickly through the north. Venice revolted against its Austro-Hungarian rulers a few days later and established a new government, the Republic of Saint Mark, and elected a president, Daniele Manin. But the revolutions in both Milan and Venice needed support in case of an Austro-Hungarian counterattack. The two cities asked the king of Sardinia for protection.

That king, Charles Albert, saw that revolution provided an opportunity to expand his influence in northern Italy. He declared war on Austria-Hungary. At first, the war went very well, but then the Austro-Hungarians regrouped and defeated the King's army. However, when

Mazzini: Republic and Unity

During the course of the revolution in Genoa in 1830, a young man, Giuseppe Mazzini, was arrested. Mazzini, who was only 25 at the time, was already the head of the local *Carbonari*. A student of literature and law at the university, Mazzini was also an active revolutionary, committed to the reestablishment of the Republic of Genoa.

Mazzini's punishment for leading the revolt was exile, and he left Genoa for Paris. In the French capital he created a new revolutionary group, Young Italy, whose members could not be over the age of forty.

Mazzini thought long and hard about the failure of revolution in Italy since 1815. He concluded that as long as foreign countries (especially Austria-Hungary) decided to send armies to suppress change in Italy, the local uprisings of individual cities had no chance of success. Only in unity could the movement for change survive against the military strength of Austria-Hungary. It was Mazzini who first connected political change to unity, and the slogan for the supporters of Young Italy was "Republic and Unity." Mazzini sketched out his ideas in 1831:

> Young Italy is *Republican* . . . because theoretically every nation is destined by the law of God and humanity to form a free and equal community of brothers; and the republic is the only form of government that insures this future. Because all true sovereignty resides

Charles Albert opened peace negotiations with Austria-Hungary, his own citizens, in the capital city of Turin, rose up in revolt and forced the King off his throne. They established a constitutional monarchy under a new ruler, Victor Emmanuel II.

essentially in the nation, the sole progressive and continuous interpreter of the supreme moral law.

Young Italy is *Unitarian* because without unity there is no true nation. Because without unity there is no real strength; and Italy, surrounded as she is by powerful, united and jealous nations, has need of strength before all things. . . .

Young Italy must be neither a sect nor a party, but a faith and an apostolate. As the precursors of Italian regeneration, it is our duty to lay the first stone of its religion.*

Unfortunately, when it came to revolution, Mazzini was much better at thinking than acting. Over the next ten years, Mazzini's own revolutions failed in Genoa, Savoy, Piedmont, and elsewhere in the center and south of Italy. Despite talk about the people of Italy, Mazzini never made contacts with the peasantry, who represented the vast majority of the Italians.

Mazzini's moment of glory came as one of the presidents of the Roman Republic. His greatest achievement, however, was the influence that his call to unity had on the other thinkers of the *Risorgimento*.

*From: Shepard B. Clough and Salvatore Saladini, editors, *A History of Modern Italy: Documents, Readings and Commentary.* (New York: Columbia University Press, 1968), pp. 35–36.

Over the next months, Austria-Hungary's armies defeated all the northern revolutions. A revolt in Naples was also suppressed. In Rome, a popular insurrection overthrew the Pope and declared a republic; however, an international army led by the French quickly defeated the Roman Republic and reinstalled the Pope in 1849.

At the end of the 1850's, though local uprisings had installed short-lived governments in many cities, only in the Kingdom of Sardinia (which included the area around Piedmont) did a king rule with a constitution. Piedmont became the model for the unification of Italy, which began ten years later.

Unification: Cavour Finds the Answer

After fourteen centuries of foreign occupation and forty-five years of revolution, Italy was created in the remarkably short period of two years. The architect of unification was the prime minister of the Kingdom of Sardinia, a brilliant diplomat from Piedmont named Count Camillo Cavour. Cavour solved the riddle of Italian unity by finding a foreign power, France, whose new leader, Louis Napoleon (the nephew of Napoleon Bonaparte I) wanted to see Austro-Hungarian influence in northern Italy restricted. The best way to do this, Cavour argued, was to help the Kingdom of Sardinia to expand.

The Piedmontese and the French declared war on Austria-Hungary in 1859. After major battles in the north, Piedmont gained Lombardy from the Austro-Hungarian rulers. The war, however, had unexpected consequences. The people in Tuscany revolted again, overthrew the Grand Duke, and asked to be annexed to Piedmont. Parma and Modena soon followed. The Papal State of Bologna also rebelled and asked to be absorbed by Piedmont.

A limited war for the expansion of Piedmont suddenly became a

SWITZERLAND

AUSTRIA

SAVOY
*To France
1860*

TRENTINO
1919

LOMBARDY
1859

VENETIA
1866

PIEDMONT

FRANCE

TRIESTE
1919

NICE
*To France
1860*

PARMA
MODENA
LUCCA
1860

UNIFICATION
OF ITALY
1859 - 1870

Kingdom of the Two Sicilies (1860)

Kingdom of Sardinia

Regions aquired by World War 1

0		50		100			150	miles
0	50	100	150	200	km			

TUSCANY
1860

CORSICA
*To France
1768*

PAPAL STATES
1860

Adriatic
Sea

ROME 1870

SARDINIA

Tyrrhenian
Sea

MEDITERRANEAN
SEA

SICILY

AFRICA

Giuseppe Garibaldi (1807–1882) was first a revolutionary with Mazzini and later an army general under Cavour. His conquests brought the South into the new Kingdom of Italy. This painting shows him in uniform during the battle for Naples in 1860. The Bettmann Archive

major revolution. This development frightened the French leader Louis Napoleon, who quickly brought an end to the war with Austria-Hungary. It took several months for an international congress of nations to decide on the fate of Italy, but the Kingdom of Sardinia was finally allowed to annex Parma, Modena, and Bologna in exchange for giving up Nice and Savoy to France. The first stage of Italian unification was complete.

At the same time, peasant uprisings in Sicily created a crisis for the

Garibaldi: Hero of Two Worlds

Garibaldi's life was that of a revolutionary. Born in 1807 in the city of Nice (which was then a part of the Kingdom of Sardinia), he entered Mazzini's Young Italy group in the early 1830's. Garibaldi carried his political beliefs into the Piedmontese navy, but when an insurrection failed in 1833, he fled for the French port of Marseilles.

Three years later, Garibaldi left for South America. He fought in Uruguay's war for independence against Argentina and eventually rose to the position of commander-in-chief of the armed forces. Garibaldi became one of the heros of that war. In the midst of the fighting, Garibaldi, short on money, had to provide clothes for his troops. He obtained shirts used by butchers, already stained by blood, and had them dyed red. From that moment, red became the color of revolution.

Garibaldi returned to Italy and helped organize the defense of the Roman Republic in 1849. He later enrolled in the army of the king of Sardinia and raised a volunteer force, which fought with distinction in the war against Austria-Hungary in 1859. Garibaldi's fame was guaranteed with the expedition to Sicily in 1860.

Garibaldi inspired people wherever he went. A Swiss writer commented in 1860 on the effect of "The General's" appearance in Sicily:

> Today, I managed to get quite close and hear his speech. He is quite admirable, like a lion, with a fine voice, thick-set body and limbs. He must be terrible when angry, but in repose his eyes are quiet and his smile soft. More than a genius, he is an apostle, a man of faith, strength and fearlessness, a miracle worker. He would be someone who in a storm could leave his ship and walk on the water. He proceeds straight ahead to fulfill his mission, to follow his star like a true conqueror. . . .*

*From: Denis Mack-Smith, *The Making of Italy, 1780–1860* (New York: Harper & Row, 1968), pp. 320.

ruler of the Kingdom of the Two Sicilies in Naples. Victor Emmanuel II, the King of Sardinia in Turin, decided to send a limited military expedition to Sicily in order to see what might be gained for Piedmont. Giuseppe Garibaldi, a general in the Piedmontese army, was put at the head of a volunteer force of one thousand (the *Mille*). Dressed in bright-red shirts, they set sail for Sicily in May 1860.

Dictator of Sicily

Garibaldi found the island in chaos, as centuries of peasant grievances erupted in riots throughout Sicily. The troops of the king of Naples were already hard-pressed by the peasants, and Garibaldi's *Mille* were enough to tip the scales of battle. He scored victory after victory. Garibaldi seized the capital city of Palermo in June 1860 and had conquered the rest of the island by August. He declared himself "Dictator of Sicily." Garibaldi then crossed the narrow Straits of Messina to the southern mainland and quickly fought his way north. In September, the king of Naples fled the city, and Garibaldi took over all of the south of Italy. He proclaimed that his next stop would be Rome.

Count Cavour, the Piedmontese Prime Minister, had never trusted Garibaldi. After the victory of the *Mille* in the south, Cavour grew worried about Garibaldi's loyalty to King Victor Emmanuel II. Cavour decided that Garibaldi had to be stopped short of Rome. The Prime Minister convinced the King to send the army to challenge Garibaldi (whose forces had grown to over twenty thousand). On their way south, the King's army passed through the Papal States of the Marches and Umbria and annexed those areas to the Kingdom of Sardinia.

A scene from the market in Palermo, Sicily, in the late 1800's. The man in the foreground is milking a goat. The Bettmann Archive

King Victor Emmanuel II and Garibaldi met on the fields near Teano at the end of October 1860. No one was quite sure whether the king would be forced to fight Garibaldi. But no shots were fired. Garibaldi voluntarily turned over the lands he had conquered to Victor Emmanuel. The Kingdom of Sardinia now included all of southern Italy. Six months later, in March 1861, Victor Emmanuel declared the lands conquered in 1859 and 1860 to be part of a new country, the Kingdom of Italy.

"Well, We've Finally Made It!"

Two areas on the Italian peninsula were still not part of the new kingdom. They were both added over the next decade. In 1866, Italy again went to war against Austria-Hungary, this time for control over the northeastern region called the Veneto. Though Italy lost that war, its ally in the north, Prussia, thoroughly defeated Austria-Hungary. The Italians attended the peace conference and gained the Veneto for the Kingdom of Italy.

Only Rome remained independent. This was the city of the Catholic Church, and the Pope's safety was guaranteed by France and its powerful army. For many years the Kingdom of Italy left the delicate issue of Rome alone. A war between France and Prussia in 1870, however, changed the Italians' attitude. The French pulled their troops out of Rome to aid in the defense against Prussia. This left the papal city virtually defenseless. The King of Italy took advantage of this opportunity. On September 20, 1870, Italian artillery blasted a hole in the wall of Rome, and the King's troops invaded the city. After a battle lasting only a few hours, Rome was conquered by the Italians. It became the capital of the Kingdom of Italy in 1871. Pope Pius IX declared himself a "prisoner of the Vatican." For the rest of his life (he died in 1878), he refused to recognize the Kingdom of Italy.

Late in the fall of 1870, Victor Emmanuel II himself finally arrived in the newly captured city of Rome. Looking out from his royal carriage, the King declared, "Well, we've finally made it!" However, Victor Emmanuel spoke not in Italian, but in the dialect of Piedmont.

The King's phrase reveals a major problem facing the new Kingdom of Italy. Not even the King of Italy spoke the Italian language as his native tongue. A single country had been created, but it was far from being a unified nation. Italy had been a peninsula divided and separated since the fall of the Roman Empire in the late 400's. Fourteen centuries of history could not be overcome by the work of Piedmont in one decade. The people living in the new kingdom, mostly peasants, spoke different languages, had different customs and came from different societies. The North was vastly different from the South. The Catholic Church refused to recognize the new nation. There was still no real sense of "Italy." As one of the first politicians in the new kingdom stated, "We have created Italy—now we need to create Italians." In some ways, the efforts to create Italians continue today, well into the twentieth century.

The Twentieth Century

In 1870, Italy was a nation of approximately 25 million people. Most Italians were poor peasants who could neither read nor write. They worked long hours in the fields and lived hard, often miserable lives. Few peasants owned their own land, and the labor contracts for sharecroppers and field workers favored the landowners. Agriculture was far more productive in the northern and central areas of Italy than in the South, where poverty and misery were commonplace. None of Italy's 20 million peasants could vote.

Italian peasants had one solution to their problems at hand: emigration. Tens of thousands of peasants, mostly from the poorest regions of the South, abandoned Italy each year, hoping for a better life elsewhere. Some traveled to other European countries, but many crossed

Wash day in the town of Ajaccio on the island of Corsica.   The Bettmann Archive

the Atlantic to Argentina, Brazil, the United States, or Canada. The numbers grew, with 500,000 leaving each year by the early 1900's. Forty years after unification, in 1914, 5 to 6 million Italians had left their country and were living outside of Italy.

The rulers of Italy had little interest in the problems of the peasants. Wealthy and educated men, mostly from northern cities, led Italy. These legislators were preoccupied with questions of their own political power. Government was based on weak alliances among many different groups, and allegiances constantly changed in Parliament. From 1870 to 1900, thirteen prime ministers tried to lead the government. Most lasted in office only two years, resigning when the divisions in the Parliament led to a vote of no confidence in their government. (For more on Italian parliamentary government, see Chapter VIII.) The result was political instability. Italian politicians could agree only to disagree, and they paid little attention to the real problems of their country. Peasants and politicians lived in two different worlds within the same nation.

Smokestacks

In the decades around the turn of the century, the industrialization of the Italian economy began. Geography favored the growth of industry in the North: Closer to industrial areas elsewhere in Europe and blessed with abundant rivers for water power, Piedmont and Lombardy were the first regions to develop new techniques of production. The first major factories appeared: the Pirelli rubber factory (1872), the FIAT automobile plant in Turin (1880's), and the Breda steelworks (1886). By the turn of the century, Italy had an "industrial triangle" made up of the cities of Turin, Milan, and Genoa. Peasants moved from the countryside to the towns to work in the new industries.

However, when rural peasants became industrial workers, they only traded one set of problems for another. Living conditions in the new northern cities were terrible, with overcrowding and poor sanitation. In the first factories, a grueling pace, long hours, and very low pay made work just as hard as labor in the countryside. Most of the early industrial labor force was women and children, working the longest hours for the least money.

Socialism and Social Reform

The old problems facing Italian peasants and the new ones of industrial workers required solutions. Two social reform movements addressed these issues. One was led by the Italian socialists. They organized Italy's first trade unions

and negotiated with factory owners and landowners for better pay and working conditions. The socialists also formed a political party in 1892 and soon afterward began to elect representatives to the Italian Parliament. These men introduced legislation to aid the common people of Italy. Both the Socialist Party and the trade unions grew as workers and peasants joined.

The Catholic Church also sponsored a social reform movement. In the 1890's, the Church actively called for the improvement of working conditions in the factories and living conditions in the cities. The Church's network of charitable organizations helped many of the most needy. But because the Church had still not recognized the Italian State, the pope would not permit Catholics from this reform movement to be candidates for the Italian Parliament. This limited the effectiveness of Catholic social reform.

Not all politicians were insensitive to the plight of the workers and peasants. Some did try to help. Giovanni Giolitti, the most prominent politician from 1900 to 1922, introduced a number of important social and civic reforms. But his measures met with strong opposition by the conservatives in the Parliament, and never received the full support of the Italian socialists.

Giolitti's greatest reform was a 1912 law that granted the right to vote to all adult men in Italy. Elections came the following year. The Italian Socialist Party received 25 percent of the national vote. Traditional politicians grew deeply worried by the strength of the socialists.

War and Peace

In the summer of 1914, war broke out between Austria-Hungary and Serbia, a small country near the Adriatic Sea. This local conflict quickly developed into the First World War, which involved most of the countries of Europe. Italy, however, pledged neutrality when the war began.

A group of men within the Italian government disagreed with the policy of neutrality. They thought that war would allow Italy to gain new land from Austria-Hungary in the north and along the eastern shores of the Adriatic Sea. These politicians began to negotiate with both sides in the First World War. England, France, and Russia promised the land these Italian leaders wanted. Italy signed a secret alliance and declared war on Austria-Hungary in April 1915.

Italy was thoroughly unprepared to fight a modern, industrial war, however. The troops were poorly trained and equipped. The war was fought under very difficult conditions in the foothills and at high elevations in the Alps. A quick victory proved impossible, so both the Italians and the Austro-Hungarians dug trenches and fortified their lines. For the next two years, fierce battles over a few hundred yards of land cost the lives of thousands of soldiers. In October 1917, the Austro-Hungarians (with German help) broke through the Italian front lines near the village of Caporetto. In only one week, Italy lost most of the Veneto. During the final year of the war, 1918, the Italians advanced slowly back toward their original positions. When they crossed into Austro-Hungarian territory in the autumn, the war ended. A truce was declared on November 4, 1918.

Disaster   The war was a disaster for Italy. Italy won no battles and suffered one major defeat. More than 350,000 soldiers died. The economy was in ruins and some of the richest agricultural land was severely damaged. To make matters worse, the peace treaties that ended the war granted Italy the most minimal concessions of Austro-Hungarian land: Only the northern mountain region of Trentino-Alto Adige and the northeastern corner of the Adriatic coast (including

Trieste) became a part of Italy. If Italy had just barely won the war, it had clearly lost the peace.

Dissatisfaction with the Italian government ran high immediately after the war. A group called the nationalists criticized the meager concessions of land that Italy obtained. They considered the peace treaty a "national humiliation" and called for the government to take action.

The Italian Socialist Party protested as well. The Socialists condemned the war as a serious mistake. They also talked of the need to nationalize the factories, the banks, and the land for the good of Italian workers and peasants. In the first elections after the war (1919), an even greater number of people voted for the Socialists: 32 percent of the national vote. The Socialists became the largest party in the Italian Parliament.

The traditional leaders of Italy feared the rise of socialism. They began to look for ways to block the Socialist Party and satisfy the nationalists. Factory owners, bankers, and landholders, equally threatened by socialism, also searched for someone to stop the Socialists.

Mussolini

The loudest voice condemning socialism and supporting the nationalists was that of Benito Mussolini. Mussolini had himself been a Socialist in his youth. Expelled from the party in 1914 for supporting Italy's entry into the war, Mussolini retained a deep hatred of his former allies. A veteran of the First World War, Mussolini also despised the Socialists' antiwar policies and condemned the terms of the peace treaty.

In 1919, Benito Mussolini became the leader of a movement called Fascism. It is very difficult to define Fascism because its own supporters—called the Fascists—never agreed themselves on what their movement represented. Nonetheless, Fascism in Italy showed some con-

Benito Mussolini, the Fascist dictator of Italy, speaks at a ceremonial occasion in the 1930's. UPI/Bettmann Newsphotos

sistent features during the years from 1919 to 1943. First, Fascism was anti-socialist. The Fascists believed that socialism would ruin Italy. Fascism was also a strong nationalist movement, which means that its supporters wanted to expand the country's influence in the world and conquer new territories for Italy. Third, Fascism was authoritarian, which means that the movement opposed democracy. The Fascists preferred dictatorship, or rule by a single individual, to rule by the people. Finally, Fascism was always violent. Fascists praised war, battle, and death. Fascism was never a movement of peace.

Mussolini on Fascism   At the height of his power, in 1935,

Mussolini offered a definition of fascism.

Fascism . . . believes neither in the possibility nor the utility of perpetual peace. It thus repudiates the doctrine of Pacifism—born of renunciation of the struggle and an act of cowardice in the face of sacrifice. War alone brings up to its highest tension all human energy and puts the stamp of nobility upon the peoples who have the courage to meet it. All other trials are substitutes, which never really put men into the position where they have to make the great decision: the alternative of life or death.

Fascism combats the whole complex system of democratic ideology and repudiates it. . . . Fascism denies that the majority, by the simple fact that it is a majority, can direct human society; it denies that numbers alone can govern by means of a periodical consultation, and it affirms the immutable, beneficial and fruitful inequality of mankind, which can never be permanently leveled through the mere operation of a mechanical process such as universal suffrage.

For Fascism, the growth of empire, that is to say the expansion of the nation, is an essential manifestation of vitality. . . . Peoples which are rising . . . are always imperialist; any renunciation is a sign of decay and of death. Fascism is the doctrine best adapted to represent the tendencies and the aspirations of a people, like the people of Italy, who are rising again after many centuries of abasement and foreign servitude. But empire demands discipline, the coordination of all forces and a deeply felt sense of duty and sacrifice. . . . Never before has the nation stood more in need of authority, of direction, and of order.*

Blackshirts   The first Fascists were men like Mussolini whose opposition to the Socialists led them to violence. The Fascists—also called the Blackshirts because of their uniform—vandalized the build-

*From: Nathanael Greene, editor, *Fascism: An Anthology*. (New York: Crowell, 1968), pp. 41–45.

ings of the Socialist Party, destroyed its printing presses, burned Socialist newspapers, and occasionally murdered their opponents. In many areas, the police, who quietly opposed socialism as well, ignored the violence of the Blackshirts. From 1919 to 1922, the Socialists suffered at the hands of the Fascists in the center and north of Italy.

At the same time, the Italian government was in a terrible state. Severe economic problems after the war required urgent solutions. However, five governments rose and fell in only four years. Italian politics had reached a deadlock: The Socialists refused to enter the government, betting that the next elections would give them even more support, while the traditional leaders of Italy would not invite the Socialists into the government, fearing the loss of their power. The only alternative for Italy's politicians was to search for new, anti-Socialist partners.

That meant Mussolini and his Fascist Party. In the 1921 elections, the Fascists obtained just 7 percent of the national vote and thirty-five seats (out of over four hundred) in the Parliament by campaigning on a nationalist and anti-Socialist platform.

The political crisis in Italy reached its peak in October 1922. Though his movement was small, Mussolini knew that Fascism was indispensable to the government. He decided to force the issue. Mussolini called on the Fascists to prepare for a revolution. Approximately 25,000 Blackshirts converged on Rome, ready to seize power for Fascism. This was the "March on Rome," the first time that Mussolini had threatened the government with violence. Faced with the prospect of an armed uprising and seeing the general acceptance of Fascism by Italy's traditional leaders, King Victor Emmanuel III asked Mussolini to become the Prime Minister. Mussolini eagerly accepted the King's offer. On October 30, 1922, he formed the first Fascist government of Italy.

Fascism in Power

Over the next few years, Mussolini used the powers of government to consolidate Fascism in Italy. He placed his supporters in government positions. He continued to play on the fear of Socialism and he promised strong and stable government for Italy. When the country went to the polls in April 1924, Mussolini again unleashed the Black-shirts. They beat up the opponents of Fascism, destroyed thousands of ballots, and falsified the counting of the votes. The results gave the Fascists nearly two thirds of the vote. The election was a fraud, but only a minority cared. Democracy was about to disappear in Italy.

Il Duce　　The Fascists obtained control of the Parliament in 1925. Mussolini used his majority to pass new laws that changed his government into a dictatorship. Parliament gave Mussolini expanded executive and legislative powers. He eliminated a free press and instituted strict government censorship. He made all other political parties illegal and disbanded the trade unions. Mussolini recalled all the passports in Italy and allowed only those people approved by the Fascists to travel outside of the country. By 1927, Mussolini was much more than a prime minister: He was *il Duce* (the Leader).

Many of Mussolini's opponents were arrested and convicted of treason. They often spent long periods in jails. Others were forced to leave the country or sent into exile in some of the most backward areas of southern Italy. Some of the Duce's opponents were murdered. Many of the other leaders in Italy chose to retire from politics. In these ways, Mussolini silenced the voices of opposition to Fascism. That silence was all that was needed to install a dictatorship in a peasant country like Italy.

Mussolini made certain not to challenge the monarchy or the Church in Italy. The *Duce* made no move against the King; Victor Emmanuel

Antonio Gramsci

Antonio Gramsci, a member of the Italian Communist Party, was one of the most prominent opponents to Mussolini. Elected as a Deputy to the Parliament in 1924, he objected to Mussolini's antidemocratic policies. Gramsci was arrested in 1926 and brought to court for treason against the state. His real crime was the refusal to accept the Fascist dictatorship. The state prosecutor warned the judge of the threat that a man like Gramsci posed: "We must stop this brain from working for twenty years." Convicted, Gramsci was sentenced to prison, where he remained for a decade.

Gramsci wrote extensively while in jail. He thought long and hard about why communism had failed and why Fascism had succeeded in Italy. The result was the *The Prison Notebooks*, one of the most important contributions to social theory in the twentieth century. Even a Fascist jail did not stop Gramsci from working, though the difficult life in prison ruined his health and led to his death in 1937.

held on to his throne until 1946. Mussolini also gained the Pope's recognition of the Kingdom of Italy. This achievement brought Mussolini a great amount of support from Catholics in the country and began a seven-year period, 1929–1936, during which Mussolini's popularity was at its height.

The Years of Fascism

Several programs of the Fascist government found favor with the Italians. Mussolini provided public works projects that kept many people employed during the worst years of the Great Depression in the early 1930's. The Fascist state financed major agricultural initiatives, including the draining of marshlands and their conversion to productive farming. Mussolini established sports clubs for children and social clubs for workers. The Fascists gave Italy stable government: Mussolini led the country from 1922 to 1943, the longest

Church and State Under Fascism

Mussolini's greatest diplomatic achievement was the reconciliation of church and state. By the late 1920's, the time was right for an agreement between the Vatican and the Kingdom of Italy: The old issues that had kept the Church hostile to Italy had died down over the six decades since unification. However, it was Mussolini who officially tied the Catholic Church to the Kingdom of Italy.

This "peace treaty," called the Lateran Pacts, was signed in February 1929. Mussolini offered Pope Pius XI a vast sum of money as compensation for the land lost by the Church during unification. The Fascist leader also committed the state to an annual contribution toward the Church's expenses (that payment ended only in 1988). The *Duce* established Catholicism as Italy's official religion and made instruction in the Catholic faith part of the Italian state school curriculum. Finally, Mussolini granted the Church the status of an independent country within the city of Rome.

In return, the Church recognized the Italian state and its government. Despite the appearance of major concessions to the Church, Mussolini was the real winner with the Lateran Pacts. He put an end to the sixty-year religious division in Italy that dated from the seizure of Rome in 1870. This gained him the support of Catholics in Italy and throughout the world. The Lateran Pacts also insured the Vatican's silence in later years, when Italy went to war as an ally of Germany and when the Nazis murdered millions of Jews and others they disliked.

rule in Italy's contemporary history.

Mussolini also satisfied those in Italy who wanted the country to expand. In the mid-1920's, Italian troops completed the conquest of Libya (begun in 1911). In October 1935, the *Duce* launched an invasion of Ethiopia, in east Africa. The war lasted nearly three years and was won only when the Italian Army used poison gas against the native Africans. Adding Somalia to Italy's other territories in Africa, Mussolini established, as he liked to say, a "Second Roman Empire."

At the same time, Fascism was a disaster for Italy. Mussolini's dictatorship took away the citizens' right to vote for twenty years. An entire generation of Italians grew up without learning to think or speak for themselves. Foreign policy under Mussolini isolated Italy in the world community, leaving the country with only one, very dangerous ally: Nazi Germany.

Another Terrible War

Mussolini's decision to take Italy into the Second World War destroyed the Fascist dictatorship. Determined not to miss an opportunity to gain new territory for Italy, Mussolini declared war on France in the spring of 1940. That part of the war was short, because the French had already been defeated by Hitler's Germany. Italy won, and gained a small amount of land.

Unfortunately for Italy, this shallow victory was the country's only success in the Second World War. The Italian occupation of Greece and Albania in the fall of 1940 turned into a major defeat. The *Duce*'s decision to join Hitler in an invasion of the Soviet Union in 1941 ended in catastrophe: Only 30,000 of the more than 200,000 Italian soldiers who fought their way toward Moscow returned home. By 1943, the British and Americans had conquered all of Italy's colonies in Africa.

The Italian military venture was a disaster.

The situation was grim on the home front, too. Allied aircraft began to bomb northern industrial cities in 1943. Damage was substantial, several thousand Italians died, many more lost their homes, and factory production dropped. As things got worse, the government introduced strict food rationing and longer work hours. These measures only increased the Italians' discontent with Mussolini. Opposition to the war grew.

American and British troops landed on the island of Sicily in July 1943. The war was now fought on Italian soil. The military could see imminent defeat. Civilians at home protested. Voices of discontent with the war were raised within the government, too. On July 24, 1943, the Fascist Council voted no-confidence in Mussolini. The next day, King Victor Emmanuel III summoned Mussolini to his palace and dismissed him as the Prime Minister. The *Duce* was arrested. Fascism had fallen overnight.

Partisans and Armies

A military government replaced Fascism, but it lasted only a short while. When the Allies announced the terms of a peace settlement with Italy in September, the Germans immediately invaded the country. They rescued Mussolini from a mountaintop prison and reinstalled the *Duce* in another Fascist government, the Republic of Salò (named after the resort town on the shore of Lake Garda). Mussolini was only a puppet ruler, dependent on the Germans for his power. Most Italians gave up on the *Duce*.

The Germans and the Allies now fought in Italy. Caught in between were the Italian people, and there was great suffering during 1944 and 1945. Food ran short in the cities, damage and destruction spread, and more and more civilians died.

Some Italians decided to fight the Germans and the rest of Mussolini's army. They were called the *partigiani* (partisans). Their movement, the Resistance, was particularly strong in the Apennines and the foothills of the Alps. The most important political group in the Resistance was the Italian Communist Party. The partisans enjoyed

The destruction caused by the Second World War made Italy's chronic poverty only worse. After liberating the country, Allied troops remained as an administration force. Italians and Americans celebrated their victories together. UPI/Bettmann

The Holocaust in Italy

After the invasion of Italy, the Germans strictly enforced the racial laws against the Jews that Mussolini had adopted in 1938. The deportation of Italian Jews to the concentration camps in central Europe began in the autumn of 1943. However, the campaign to eliminate the Jews in Italy was largely a failure because anti-Semitism was not a part of the country's culture.

From 1943 until the end of the war, Italians helped their Jewish neighbors to hide from the Germans. An underground network aided Italian Jews in their escape to neutral Switzerland. The Nazis killed eight thousand Italian Jews during the war, approximately 10 percent of the total Jewish population. This number was much smaller than the deaths of Jews in most of the other Nazi-occupied countries of Europe.

One of the most powerful accounts of the concentration camps was written by an Italian Jew, Primo Levi. His book *Survival in Auschwitz* is a remarkable story of perseverance and even hope in some of the most desperate conditions in the twentieth century.

wide support among the people of the northern and central areas, and many of the them became Italy's new leaders at the end of the war.

The Allies made steady progress northward, occupying Naples in September 1943. They reached Rome in June 1944 and Florence in the following September. In the spring of 1945, the Allies crossed the Apennines and invaded northern Italy. The Italian partisans liberated many towns on their own. Mussolini, disguised as a common soldier, tried to escape across the border into Austria. Italian partisans discovered the *Duce* hiding in the back of a truck and shot him as a traitor to the country.

At the end of April, 1945, Italian resistance fighters captured Mussolini as he tried to escape to Austria. The Duce *was shot and his body, along with those of his mistress and closest collaborators, was put on public display for several days in Milan. This grim photograph underscores the Italians' anger at the destruction that Mussolini's war had brought to their country.* UPI/Bettmann

Peace and Poverty

Peace came to Italy at the end of April 1945. The war was finally over, but the Italians now faced staggering problems. The country had to be put back together again after four years of war. It took a decade and several hundred million dollars in United States aid from the Marshall

Plan to reconstruct. Italy remained a poor country all through the late 1940's and 1950's.

A year after the war's end, in June 1946, the Italians went to the polls. This was the first election in the history of Italy in which all adults participated, for women had been just granted the right to vote. It was also the first appearance of democracy after twenty-five years of Fascism. The Italians were asked to choose between a monarchy or a republic. They voted in favor of a republic, but only by a narrow margin (54 percent to 46 percent). The king left Italy for exile abroad.

On January 1, 1948, the new constitution for the democratic Republic of Italy went into effect. It remains one of the most liberal in all of Europe and North America. Elections in April of that year placed the government in the hands of a new political party, the Christian Democracy. The Italian Communists came in second place, the Italian Socialists third. Many smaller political parties took up seats in the Parliament as well. It was now the turn of the Republic to lead this complex country in the modern period.

Democracy
in Italy

Italy is well known for its many governments*: There have been over fifty since the end of the Second World War. This means that the average Italian government lasts a little less than one year. At first glance, then, Italy presents a picture of great political instability. No other nation in Europe or North America has had as many short-lived governments. How is it possible for Italy to continue with governments that change so frequently?

The answer to this question requires looking at the way democracy works in Italy. Understanding the country's political system is a little bit like solving a puzzle that has many pieces, few of which seem at

*A "government" in a parliamentary system is something like an "administration" in America; it refers to the group of people who *govern* with the approval of the legislature. In America a President remains in office even if another party controls Congress.

first to fit together. But three pieces of this Italian political puzzle are important. First, there is hidden stability in the Italian political system. Secondly, democracy in Italy is based on government by many different political parties. And finally, the Italian system has rested on a balance between two points of view—a Catholic one and a communist one. There is much more to democracy in Italy than just the record number of governments.

Stability

Italy actually holds two political records. In addition to having had the most governments in the post-war period, Italy is also the only Western democracy in which one political party has dominated government. That party is the nation's largest, Christian Democracy. For over forty years and in more than forty-five different governments, the Christian Democrats have led Italy. Hidden beneath the country's rapidly changing governments is the stability of Christian Democracy's rule.

Politicians in Italy also have long careers. The same men (and fewer women) have held political offices in many different Italian governments. The best example is Giulio Andreotti, a member of the Christian Democracy, who has been in all of the governments since 1947. Andreotti has held important positions in political offices such as foreign and internal affairs on many occasions. He has also been the leader of the government seven times. Andreotti's experience in government is vast—no other Western politician can match it. But Andreotti is only one example of the long political careers common in Italy. The recycling of the same people in government after government is another stabilizing element in Italian democracy.

Stability also comes from a third source. The many changes in governments are rarely due to serious political crises. Much more common in Italy is the "crisis" that is really a disagreement among political

leaders or a clash of personalities. This kind of political dispute is fairly easy to solve. The heads of political parties most often patch up their differences and form a new government, sometimes in a matter of only a few days. Occasionally, these "new" governments are exact replicas of the earlier ones. The Italians call these "photocopy governments," a term that indicates how little has changed even if a new government has formed.

Finally, the rise and fall of a government in Italy does not require the Italians to go to the polls for an election. The official legislative term is five years. During that period, there can be any number of "crises" and new governments. Only when the politicians cannot resolve the dispute on their own and the legislature is forced to end early do the Italians end a "crisis" by voting in a new legislature. Half of the legislatures in Italy have lasted their full five years, while in the same period there might have been three or even four different governments.

Stable or Stagnant?   Government dominated by the Christian Democrats, political leadership exercised by the same men and women for long periods of time, a political "crisis" that most often isn't a crisis at all, and the rise and fall of governments without the citizens being called to the polls—these four elements give Italy a particularly stable democracy, despite the great number of rapidly changing governments. Some experts consider Italy's political system to be not only stable, but stagnant. What Italy does not have is the alternation in power between different political parties common to other Western countries. This is perhaps the most peculiar aspect of the Italian system.

Political posters fill the streets in Italy at election time.   Agenzia Fotogiornalistica Cronaca Nuova/Carlo Bozzardi

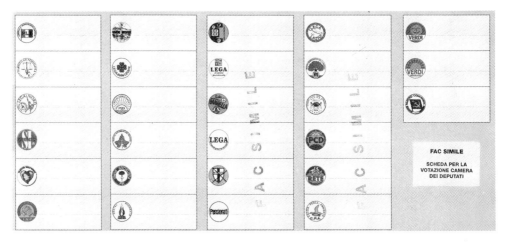

Twenty-seven political parties appeared on the ballot for national elections in April 1992. The Italians' vote of protest made the formation of a stable government coalition—Italy's major political problem for more than four decades—even more difficult.

Political Parties

Democracy in Italy works in ways very different from the American model. First, there are many different political parties in Italy. How many? The number changes from year to year, but there may be twenty or more in any national election. This large number may seem to create nothing but confusion. The situation in Italy is really simpler than it first appears—there are really only three major parties.

The largest political party in Italy is the Christian Democracy, which receives about one third of the national vote. The second-largest party is the Democratic Party of the Left (formerly the Italian Communist Party), with about 20 percent of the vote. The third major party in Italy is the Socialist Party, with almost 15 percent. Together, these three parties account for nearly two thirds of the national vote in Italy.

Four other parties are important, even though they are much smaller. There is a new fascist party (called the Italian Social Movement), which receives 5 percent of the vote, a Republican Party (4 percent), a Social-Democrat Party (3 percent), the Liberal Party (3 percent), and an ecological party, called the *Verdi* (the Greens) with 3 percent. Two new political parties appeared recently. One is called Communist Refoundation (with 6 percent of the vote). The second is the *Lega* (the League), which wants to take political power away from the central government in Rome and give it to each of the country's regions. This protest movement did very well in 1992: Its 9 percent of the vote makes the League the fourth-largest party in Italy (1992 figures).

The number and variety of parties create a very lively political scene. These parties—both large and small—represent a wide range of opinion on issues important to Italy, and most Italians find a party that matches fairly well their own ideas about government and society. This encourages the Italians to vote, and over 85 percent of the electorate

One of the newest political parties in Italy is the Verdi *("Greens"), the country's environmental movement. Their symbol is the smiling sun. Here, the* Verdi *on bicycles protest the congestion and traffic in downtown Rome.* Agenzia Fotogiornalistica Cronaca Nuova/Carlo Bozzardi

goes to the polls in national elections. This is among the highest figure in Europe and far higher than the voter turnout in the United States, which was barely over 50 percent in the 1988 presidential elections. The greatest strength of democracy in Italy is that politics continues to attract the interest and participation of its citizens.

The Art of Governing

However, the large number of parties in Italy also makes the country difficult to govern. Because votes are split among many different groups, no single political party in Italy has ever received an absolute majority (more than 50 percent) of the votes by itself. The Christian Democracy comes the closest, but its 35 percent share of the vote is still far short of the majority.

The result is that governments in Italy must be made up of alliances that bring together different parties to form the majority needed to rule the country. A government based on these alliances is called a coalition government. There is no limit to the number of parties that may make up a coalition. In theory, any combination is possible: two, three, four, five (as has recently been the case), or even more political parties.

The art of government in Italy lies in finding agreement among all the members of the potential coalition. Political leaders have to search for the right formula for their alliance. Finding a set of policies acceptable to many different parties is a difficult and time-consuming task, sometimes taking several weeks. Constructing a coalition requires cooperation and agreement among a wide range of political groups. This ensures the representation of many different opinions—the essence of democracy—within the government.

The frequent changes in government are also due to the number of political parties included in the coalitions. When one (or more) of the parties of a coalition decides that it can no longer support the common program agreed upon earlier, the coalition may no longer have enough votes to control the Parliament. If this occurs, the weakened alliance can no longer govern Italy. The parties of the coalition try to resolve their differences. If they can, the "crisis" soon passes. If not, the government must resign and a new one must form. If a solution still cannot be found, the legislature is suspended and the country goes to the polls to vote. There is no time limit placed on how long a crisis can last: Some are over within a few days while others go on for weeks and occasionally even months.

A Crisis a Year

The likelihood of disagreement is fairly high in an Italian coalition government made up of several parties. There might be a serious problem to resolve (such as finances, crime, or immigration), or the disagreement might focus on a relatively minor issue.

Italians wait for buses that always seem to be late and overcrowded. The transportation system in the major cities is one example of the general inefficiency of public services. The situation is much better in the smaller towns of the provinces. Agenzia Fotogiornalistica Cronaca Nuova/Carlo Bozzardi

In either case, the legislative affairs of the country come to a halt. And given that there is a "crisis" on the political horizon almost every year, it is very difficult for the Italian government to follow its legislative schedule and govern the country effectively. Italian politicians, as a result, have become managers rather than leaders. They are often more concerned with avoiding or resolving political "crises" than with planning for Italy's future. They prefer to postpone or avoid the difficult decisions that might create disagreement within the coalition. All of these elements make government in Italy weak and slow to take action.

Party-ocracy

The existence of so many political parties also creates an intermediate level between the citizens and government in Italy. When the Italians go to the polls, they do not vote directly for a particular government. Rather, they cast their votes for the representatives of individual political parties. These men and women serve in one of the two houses of the Italian Parliament (the Senate or the Chamber of Deputies). It is these representatives, the senators and deputies, who actually form a government. Many people consider the Italian system not a pure democracy, in which the people rule directly, but a "party-ocracy" in which the political parties are in charge of government.

The parties decide who will become the official leader of the nation, the President of the Italian Republic. The president serves a seven-year term (which may be renewed). The position is largely ceremonial (filling in for the monarchy, which was abolished in 1946), and the president's powers are not clearly defined. The President of the Republic is not elected directly by the voters of Italy; instead, he or she is elected by the votes of the Senators and Deputies. (All the presidents since 1945 have been men, although the constitution permits women to hold government offices.)

The position of leader of the Italian nation is distinct from that of the head of government. Another "president," called the President of the Council of Ministers (equivalent to the Prime Minister), leads the government and is in charge of the day-to-day business of running Italy. The President of the Council of Ministers is not directly elected by the population either, but is appointed by the President of the Republic and later confirmed in office by the political parties of the Parliament.

Though the president of the council oversees the daily activities of the government, direct control is in the hands of the ministers themselves (who are similar to secretaries of the departments in the United States government). The number of ministers varies; at this writing, there are more than thirty-two. The more important posts include the ministries of agriculture, defense, environment, finance, foreign affairs (the equivalent of the U.S. State Department), health and welfare, labor, industry, and internal affairs. Party-ocracy may be seen at work in the council of ministers as well: All the positions are divided among the political parties that form the coalition government.

Two other high public offices are important in Italy: These are the leaders of the two houses of Parliament. The President of the Senate conducts the business of that house with its 315 elected members; the President of the Chamber of Deputies oversees the work of the 630 members in the other half of Italy's Parliament. Both presidents are chosen by agreement among the political parties.

Party-ocracy, then, means government by political parties. In the Republic of Italy, when the ministries and the country's four presidents are divided up, almost every political party controls at least one office (and usually many more). The promise of a high government position to individual parties is the glue that holds coalitions together, but this mechanism may favor political loyalty instead of competence. Often the result is the appointment of poorly qualified people to positions of great responsibility. This further lessens the efficiency of government.

Christians and Communists

The process of putting together a government coalition in Italy is a complicated one. Agreement on policies and the division of government positions among parties are the two most important elements. But the possible combinations of parties and policies are still almost infinite. How has the country managed to find a formula for its coalitions over the years?

One element has remained constant for more than forty years: the exclusion of the Communists from the coalition. All of the governments since 1947 have been formed without the Italian Communist Party, or since 1991, its replacement, the Democratic Party of the Left. All of the coalitions have been led by the Christian Democracy. The last piece of the Italian political puzzle lies in the balance between these two points of view: Christian and Communist.

Christian Democracy is a political party for everyone. More Italians from all walks of life vote for the Christian Democrats than for any other single political party. This sometimes presents problems. For example, most farmers and many grocery store owners vote for the Christian Democracy; however, a program that is good for the farmers—one that keeps food prices high, for example—may be a disaster for the grocery store owner. Deciding between the two alternatives can be very difficult. When faced with this problem, Christian Democracy's leaders most often try not to choose but to wait for the problem to work itself out.

Because the Christian Democracy has been at the center of Italian government for so many years, this party's tendency not to decide has set a style of government for the nation as a whole. The inability to choose and the preference for postponement contribute to making Italian government indecisive and weak. Italy often drifts along while its politicians ignore the important issues facing the country and try to avoid hard choices for as long as possible. The result is a government that often does not lead the country, but only follows.

The permanence of the Christian Democracy in government has led the party to focus more on maintaining political power and less on the general interest of the nation. This is a common occurrence when one party dominates the political life of a country for such a long period of time. Christian Democracy is a party of favors and privileges, and it suffers from corruption and frequent scandals.

A New Party

Until 1991, the counterweight to the Christian Democracy was the Italian Communist Party. With nearly 1.5 million members and 9 million votes, Italian Communism was the largest communist party in Western Europe. It was also a democratic political party, working through the Parliament to change Italy. Communists ran in elections and served as local administrators, city mayors, senators and deputies. The Communist Party accepted private property and capitalism as the basis of the Italian economy, they welcomed Catholics into their movement, and they criticized the ex-Soviet Union for its lack of democracy.

This Italian version of Communism was so peculiar that it was thought to be communist only in name. Over the last few years, the Italian Communists decided to change even that. In 1991, they reformed their political movement, and now call it the Democratic Party of the Left (PDL). They hope that a new name and a platform of expanded civil rights and greater democratic representation will encourage more Italians to vote for their alternative to Christian Democracy. A minority of the old Communists did not agree to this change and established their own movement, Communist Refoundation. Even though under a different name, the supporters of the new Democratic Party of the Left will still counter the Catholic point of view in the traditional balance that has kept democracy in Italy going for five decades.

Festa di l'Unità

A good idea of what politics is in Italy comes from a visit to the annual gathering of the Democratic Party of the Left: the *Festa di l'Unità* (the Festival of Unity). This festival lasts for three weeks during the summer and attracts several million visitors. The emphasis at the *Festa* is on politics. Debates on subjects of current interest, with speakers from all points of view, are held nightly for the weeks of the national gathering.

But the festival is not only about politics. There are also classical music and rock-and-roll concerts, movies in large open-air theaters, art shows, ballroom dancing and disco, sports, and bookstalls. And because everything in Italy happens around the dinner table, the *Festa di l'Unità* is also famous for its food. At least fifteen different restaurants with menus from all over the world are represented; there are also standard Italian meals, pizzas, sandwiches, and bars. Combining politics with pleasure, discussing the problems of modern Italy while enjoying a delicious meal: This is the purpose of the yearly festival.

Between the Christian Democracy and the ex-Communists lies the Italian Socialist Party. The Socialists are currently part of the government coalition alongside the Christian Democrats. However, the Socialists hint that they might become partners with other parties, perhaps even the PDL, in the future. The Socialists have done very well by occupying the middle ground between the Christians and the Communists, more than doubling their share of the vote in the fifteen years since 1975. Though still smaller than either the Christian Democracy or the ex-Communists, the Socialist Party in this middle position has had a major role in the formation (and crises) of the recent governments in Italy. Whether the Italian Socialist Party will really bring substantial change to the country is uncertain. As the primary coalition partner with Christian Democracy through the 1980's, the Socialists have shown themselves quite capable of governing to their own benefit without much regard to Italy's general interest. Italian Socialism is now a party firmly of the status quo in Italy and is a political movement as unlikely as Christian Democracy to sponsor significant changes.

Threats to Italian Democracy

In the 1960's and 1970's, threats to democracy in Italy took the form of conspiracies to wrest power away from elected representatives and the Italian people.

Right-Wing Plots
The most serious of these threats arose within the political system itself. In 1964, a commander of the Italian national police, convinced that the nation was heading politically to the left (and in his view towards disaster), organized a coup against the state. The plan was discovered in time, and a right-wing takeover was prevented. However, the truth concerning the coup was hidden from the country for years, and the men responsible were never punished.

In 1981, the existence of a secret organization within the government was revealed. Called the P-2 (Propaganda-2), its 962 members were some of the most important politicians, military officers, industrialists, bankers, judges, civil servants, journalists, and police officers in the country. Fearing the political left, the P-2 infiltrated government, military, and economic circles. Most of the organization's members were forced to resign their public positions. The serious political crisis that followed forced the Christian Democracy government to resign in disgrace.

After more than ten years and many court trials, no one has yet been found guilty for the right-wing terrorist bombing of the Bologna train station in 1980. This woman's sign, "85 Victims Waiting for Justice," reveals the frustration with the inability to solve this crime. Agenzia Fotogiornalistica Cronaca Nuova/Carlo Bozzardi

From 1969 to the early 1980's, Italy was also threatened by a wave of terrorism. Neo-fascist terrorists, convinced that Italy needed a stronger and more authoritarian state, attacked innocent civilians. These small groups hoped that the fear of more terrorism would push the population to demand a stronger government. Bombs planted by right-wing terrorists exploded in crowded buildings and in train cars, killing many people. The most notorious act of neo-fascist terrorism came in August 1980 when a suitcase with high explosives killed eighty and injured another two hundred in the waiting room at the Bologna train station.

Left-Wing Terror
Left-wing terrorism also plagued Italy in the 1970's. The best known of the many groups was the Red Brigades. In an attempt to weaken the state, the Red Brigades injured, kidnapped, and often killed prominent Italians and representatives of the government—industrialists, judges, bureaucrats, journalists, police, and military officers. In 1978, the Red Brigades kidnapped the leader of the Christian Democracy, Aldo Moro, held him prisoner in an apartment in Rome, and finally assassinated him two months later.

Police investigation brought most of the left-wing terrorists to trial. Some fled into exile abroad rather than face arrest, but many were sentenced to long prison terms. The record against the right-wing terrorists, however, has been very poor. Despite several trials, there have been few convictions for acts of neo-fascist terrorism. The country's intelligence services themselves have been linked with right-wing terrorism. The truth may never come to light, but the suspicion that some people in government institutions aided neo-fascist terrorists has deeply disturbing implications for Italian democracy.

Contemporary terrorism from both the far right and the far left, lasting for over a decade, shook the foundations of Italian democracy. In a generally nonviolent society like Italy, political terrorism was horrifying. Fourteen thousand acts of terrorism and over five hundred deaths took place between the late 1960's and the early 1980's. Only under Mussolini and the Fascists had Italy suffered such widespread terrorism. Unlike in 1922, however, the Italians survived the 1970's terrorist crisis, rejecting violence as a means of change and at the same time maintaining their democratic institutions and civil rights.

Reform

There are many proposals for reform of Italian democracy. Most of these ideas focus on ways to modify the party-ocracy system. Changes in the electoral laws, more avenues for direct democracy, and more clearly defined responsibilities are the most popular proposals for limiting the power of the parties. Some of these reforms have quite a bit of support, especially the call for the direct election of the President of the Republic.

Italy has always been a great inventor in the field of politics. Throughout the centuries, from the days of the Roman Empire to the period of the Renaissance city-states, through unification and finally even during the Fascist dictatorship, Italy has been a laboratory for the political experiments of all Western civilization.

And the tests continue today. The Italian political laboratory has many problems, and many reforms are needed. But the overall results are good. Democracy is firmly in place in Italy. Citizens actively participate in the political system. Traditions of compromise and negotiation are the established foundations of Italian politics. Government rests much more on cooperation than on conflict, and political opponents work together each day to pass legislation and administer the nation. These are the highlights of Italian-style democracy, one of the most dynamic democratic systems in the world today.

Work and Play

Italy is a prosperous nation. In the mid-1980's, it became the third richest country in Western Europe and the fifth among the world's most wealthy industrialized nations. Behind this recent leap forward stands the work that Italians do.

Nearly 24 million people (out of a total population of just under 57 million) are employed in modern Italy (1989 figures). Almost 9 million workers (more than one third) are women. Men and women who work in agriculture make up almost 10 percent of the total labor force; industry accounts for 32 percent, and the service sector (jobs in sales and the professions) for 59 percent. Unemployment, the number of people unable to find jobs, is currently 12 percent.

North and South

These are average national statistics. Hidden behind the figures are the regional variations between the many different Italys on the peninsula. The biggest differences are between northern and southern Italy. With more people at work and more industry, the North is richer than the South. The five wealthiest regions in Italy are all northern, while the five poorest regions of Italy are all in the South. The average annual per capita (per person) national income is 13.3 million lire (around $11,500). The northern region of Lombardy, around the city of Milan, has the highest per capita yearly income, nearly 22.5 million lire (or approximately $19,500), while the southern region of Calabria has the lowest per capita income of 9.5 million lire (or approximately $8,200). The effects of these differences are explored in the next chapter.

Regional variations in unemployment are also part of this alarming picture of the different Italys. But the real employment situation may be a bit different from what these figures suggest. Throughout Italy, and particularly in the South, there is a "hidden" economy, made up of people whose work is not counted by those who compile the official statistics. While some of this "hidden" work is carried out by illegal immigrants to Italy, most is done by Italians who are not officially hired, but who receive a cash wage for their work. The official system does not track the economic activity of these people, who are really at work but often appear in government statistics as "unemployed."

In the mid-1980's, economic experts devised a statistical model that estimated the contribution of Italy's "hidden" economy to the nation's wealth. They determined that these hidden jobs account for around 25 percent of Italy's overall economic activity. This estimate moved Italy up into the ranks of the wealthiest European nations, pushing the United Kingdom out of the number-three position. The English have complained about what they consider the unreliability of these figures ever since.

An Economic Miracle

The nature of work in Italy has undergone a revolution in the post-war period. The most important change has been the decline of agriculture in the overall economic picture. As recently as the 1950's, over 40 percent of Italians made their living off the land. Peasants, sharecroppers, and small family farms accounted for most of the work and most of the wealth in Italy.

But in a period of only fifteen years, ending in the 1960's, Italy went through an "economic miracle." Having recovered from the war with the help of United States aid, Italians began to push their economy in new directions. Most important was the rapid spread of industry throughout the North. Factories had appeared in northern Italy before the twentieth century, but Italy did not become an industrial nation until the 1960's. Most of this development was concentrated in the area between the cities of Turin, Milan, and Genoa—Italy's "Industrial Triangle."

The best symbol of industrialization and the economic miracle was the FIAT automobile factory in the city of Turin. FIAT (which stands for the *Fabbrica Industriale Automobile di Turino*, or in English, the Turin Automobile Industrial Factory) grew enormously and is now Europe's largest car manufacturer, employing 300,000 people.

Historically, Italy's wealth came from the land. Even today, its primary agricultural crops remain those of the past: wheat, rice, grapes, olives, and citrus fruits. But thanks to the economic miracle, most of Italy's prosperity today comes from industry. The principal industrial products include automobiles, machinery, chemicals, rubber products, textiles, and shoes.

Old Ways in a New Italy

Industrialization brought important changes to the country. Italy had been a nation of peasants and a country of small farm villages for centuries. Suddenly, in less than one generation, Italy became an industrial and urban society. More Italians now work in factories than in the fields; more people live in cities than ever before. Despite these changes, the traditions of a peasant agricultural society live on today in modern Italy. Old customs and an older outlook on the world, common to rural cultures, are still found even in the most advanced areas of contemporary Italian life. The maintenance of a peasant culture in a new, urban society is part of the fascination of modern Italy.

Industrialization also helped to create a unified Italy. Most of the new workers for northern industry came from the South. Attracted by jobs and decent wages, tens of thousands of southern Italians left their homes in Sicily, the Basilicata, and Calabria and traveled with their families to Piedmont and Lombardy. The southern immigrants built homes on the outskirts of northern industrial cities. Their new life was a difficult one that included economic hardship and discrimination. For years, the southerners were considered outsiders because they represented a foreign population that had suddenly appeared in the North. Within a generation, however, these southern Italians had integrated into the life and society of the North. By the 1970's, the great migrations started to blend North and South into a single nation.

Over the past two decades industry has lost its predominance as the economic activity employing the most Italians. What has risen in its place is the service sector: shops of all sorts, professions (lawyers, doctors, dentists), restaurants, hotels, and tourism. Three out of five Italians now work in service-related jobs. In the shift from agriculture to industry to services, Italy has followed closely the general trend in Western Europe and North America.

Women at Work

One aspect of work that did not change during the years of the "miracle" was women's employment in the Italian economy. Despite the industrialization and urbanization of Italy, the percentage of women in the work force has remained remarkably constant, at around one third of the total, since 1960. The changing nature of women's work followed the development of the national economy. Fewer women are now employed in agriculture (down 2 percent from 1960), more in industry (up 3 percent), and many more in the service sector (up 6 percent).

Legislation has helped to keep the employment of women in Italy at a constant level. The Italian Constitution of 1948 prohibits discrimination on the basis of sex (or on the basis of religion, political beliefs, or race). Additionally, the Constitution guarantees equal civil and economic rights to women, including the right for Italian women to receive the same wages for the same work as men.

Labor contracts in Italy also deal with the problem of Italian women who wish to be both mothers and workers. Women are given time off from their jobs with nearly full pay to deliver and raise children. Positions are held for these new mothers for up to three years until they return to the workplace. The Italian government also subsidizes an extensive network of inexpensive day-care centers for working Italian women. These are some of the most liberal maternity provisions in the world.

Workers' Rights

Workers in Italy are generally well protected. A strong trade-union movement, to which nearly 45 percent of Italian workers belong, guarantees the rights of workers. A statute of workers' rights, introduced in the early 1970's, makes it impossible to dismiss any worker without a valid reason. Unemployment benefits are generous. Salaries are tied to inflation and adjusted frequently so that wages do not fall behind the cost of living. All Italians, whether at work or not, are protected by a national health care system as well.

All of these provisions are expensive. Many are funded by the Italian state, but many others are paid for by the contributions of the employers. In some cases, the actual monthly take-home wage of an Italian worker (in 1990, approximately 1.3 million lire, or $1,200) represents approximately half of the total cost to the employer. The result is that Italian labor costs are among the highest in the world.

Small Is Beautiful?

The most striking characteristic of work in Italy is the small size of businesses. The number of small-scale enterprises is staggering: More than 2 million (or 70 percent) of all businesses have no more than three employees. Many of these are local neighborhood shops, including food, fruit, and bread stores; tobacconists; clothing, jewelry, cosmetic, and household appliances stores. These are family-owned and operated business, and they form the heart of the Italian economy.

The small business is common in industry as well. Most factories (85 percent) have fewer than ten employees, while industries with more than one hundred employees are quite few (only about 1 percent of the total number). In Italian industry, the traditional small workshop of the artisan continues to thrive today.

The artisan is a specialized craftsperson who has mastered a certain skill only after years of study and practice. Italian artisans produce fine jewelry, gold pieces, and leather goods, including gloves and bags; a tradition of fine work by artisans in these products goes back centuries. Artisans also work with metal and wood in small shops that they own themselves. They often work alone but may employ a few others,

The high quality of Italy's goods is the result of a tradition of fine work by trained and dedicated artisans. Here, a Florentine artisan puts the finishing touches on a wooden ornament. Markus Peters

An artisan working in bronze and copper outside his shop in Calabria.   ENIT, Roma

some of whom are training to learn the craft as well. The quality work of Italian artisans is world renowned.

There are both advantages and disadvantages to the small scale of the Italian economy. Because most Italians either own their own businesses or work in very small stores or workshops, they have a close relationship with their work and they find satisfaction in what they do. Small industries are also quick to react to changes in styles and tastes and can adapt their production accordingly. The tiny Italian factories are some of the most profitable and dynamic in the country.

The disadvantages are apparent, too. The distribution of goods and services through thousands of tiny shops creates high prices. The network is also quite inefficient, and particular goods are not always available in the shops. Despite these problems, most Italians are content with the system as it exists. Large department stores and supermarkets are not yet popular in Italy.

Big Business and State Corporations

Italy's huge corporations and enormous businesses are on the other extreme of the nation's economy. Italy has a high concentration of economic activity in the hands of just a few people. The FIAT automobile factory is a good example. It is the country's biggest private industry, employing several hundred thousand people and producing over 80 percent of the cars sold in Italy. FIAT is also active in space and missile technology, banking, and construction. Taken together, all of FIAT's economic activities account for over one third of all the shares traded on the Italian stock market.

The FIAT automobile factory in Turin is one of Europe's largest and most modern. The gigantic size of FIAT contrasts with the small businesses common in Italy.   FIAT

The best symbol of Italy's economic recovery in the late 1950's and 1960's was the tiny FIAT 500, the country's first affordable private car.   FIAT

Even the largest businesses in Italy are family affairs. FIAT has been owned and operated by the same family, the Agnellis, since its foundation in the 1880's. Large businesses owned by a single individual or family are also seen in the chemical industry, in rubber production, and in private television and newspaper corporations.

Big business and large-scale production allows industrial goods to be made inexpensively. The enormous concentration of economic power in only a few hands also gives the directors of Italian big business a powerful voice in political affairs. Most have close ties with government leaders and political parties. Many own their own newspapers.

Despite the existence of these giant companies, only 40 percent of Italian industrial production comes from private firms. This is the lowest percentage among all Western industrial nations. The rest comes from state-owned enterprises. The biggest is the Institute for Industrial

Reconstruction, established in 1933 under Mussolini, which expanded in the post-war period to become one of Europe's largest corporations. Through its six hundred subsidiaries, the Institute dominates Italy's iron and steel industries, shipbuilding, telecommunications, electronics, engineering, radio and television, the national airline, and most of the nation's banks. Another gigantic state-owned corporation is the National Hydrocarbon Institute, which controls the nation's petroleum company, nuclear energy facilities, and chemical industries. These two enterprises, plus other state-owned corporations, are of utmost importance in the Italian economy. They are also the sites of tremendous political battles, as the parties making up government coalitions fight to place their representatives in managerial positions.

The Environment

Environmental problems have accompanied the industrialization of Italy. The rapid development of factories and poor regulation by weak governments have resulted in serious ecological problems, especially in the North. Industrial pollutants now contaminate the drinking water in many areas of northern Italy. Almost all of Italy's coastline is threatened by industrial and chemical pollution.

Intensive agriculture in the Po River Valley has led to another environmental problem: the abuse of fertilizers and pesticides. These have not only killed fish and wildlife in that area but have also contributed to the pollution of the Adriatic Sea. Green algae, which thrive on these fertilizers, bloom in the hot summer months in the shallow waters of the Adriatic. The algae kill fish and spoil the beaches. Without adequate safeguards, the Adriatic may soon become a dead sea.

Concern about pollution led to the creation of an ecological political party, the *Verdi*. Like other Green parties in Western Europe, the *Verdi* have been active in local and national governments recently. They have

Venice

The city of Venice faces a special environmental problem: It is slowly sinking into the lagoon.

Venice is a city of islands, built on pilings driven into the sandy soil of a shallow bay. Flooding occurs when high tides and winter storms combine to push the sea out of the bay, up through the canals, and into the streets. As Venice sinks lower into the sandy bottom of the lagoon, floods become much more common. The city's main square, the Piazza San Marco, lies under water several times each year. During the floods, the Venetians move around their city by gondola (a unique boat that is the symbol of Venice) or on scaffolding raised above the water.

The efforts to save Venice have taken two forms. One is an enormous project to build a massive dam that will hold back the high tides when flooding seems likely. The second idea is to reinforce most of the city center to prevent further sinkage. Both projects are complicated and expensive, and the Italian government has not yet decided on how best to protect the city.

raised questions about a wide range of environmental issues, from agricultural and industrial pollution to hunting and radioactive waste. They promote strong environmental legislation and have begun to change the way Italians think about their land.

The *Verdi*'s most important campaign focused on the dangers of radiation in case of an accident at a nuclear power plant. Their 1987 referendum received the votes of a majority of Italians and canceled the construction of new nuclear power plants in Italy.

Three Quarters of Europe's Art

Another important sector of the contemporary Italian economy is tourism. This is particularly true in the South, where a sunny climate and hundreds of miles of beautiful coastline attract thousands of beach goers from all over Europe each summer.

Italy's cultural heritage also attracts foreign visitors. Nearly three quarters of all of Western Europe's art is in Italy. Paintings, statues, churches, and ancient ruins make Italy a nation very rich in culture.

Nearly 22 million foreign visitors travel each year to Italy to see the art or enjoy the beaches. Many Italian cities, such as Florence and Venice, depend entirely on art-related tourism. The economy of other areas, such as the Romagna region and much of the South, is based on the tourists visiting their seashores. Overall, tourism brings in over 16 trillion lire (nearly $14 billion) a year into the Italian economy.

Crowded beaches are the rule in July and August when it seems as if everyone heads to the seaside for their summer vacation. Agenzia Fotogiornalistica Cronaca Nuova/Carlo Bozzardi

Fashion and clothing is another important industry in Italy. Some of the world's top designers are Italians: Gucci, Valentino, Missoni, Fendi, and Krizia are among the most famous names. The fashion shows in Milan in the spring and fall attract buyers from around the world. Italy is known for the style and quality of its clothes, and this industry accounts for over 17 trillion lire (or nearly $15 billion) in trade each year.

Mass Tourism

Italy's pleasant summer climate and magnificent art have created a serious problem in mass tourism in recent years. Simply put, too many people want to see Italy's cultural heritage. Museums cannot handle the thousands of tourists. The narrow streets of Italy's old medieval towns were not designed for hundreds of tourist buses and automobiles.

The historic art center of Florence overflows with tourists at least half of the year. The same is true of the city of Venice, where during the tourist season the population actually doubles to eighty thousand. Smaller towns, such as Siena and Pisa, are affected too.

The result is chaos: Visitors struggle with each other to see famous paintings, the streets are too crowded for walking, hotels have no rooms, and tables are unavailable at popular restaurants. The tourists are dissatisfied and life for the permanent residents becomes impossible.

Local and national governments in Italy have failed to respond to the problems of mass tourism. Proposals to establish a daily limit on the number of visitors meet with the opposition of businesspeople who depend on the tourists for their livelihood. Unable to decide, local governments and residents can only watch an already grave problem grow more serious.

Italians filled the streets to celebrate their quarter-final victory in the 1990 World Cup Soccer Championships. Agenzia Fotogiornalistica Cronaca Nuova/Carlo Bozzardi

Immigrants and the Economy

Italy has historically been a poor, peasant country. Faced with poverty, generations of Italians left their country for a better life elsewhere. From the late 1800's through the 1950's, millions of Italians emigrated to other European countries (France, Switzerland, and Germany) or crossed the ocean to North and South America. But after 1960, the "economic miracle" put an end to mass emigration from Italy.

Modern Italy's wealth, instead, reversed the trend. Now the country's problem is the immigration of people from poorer countries *into* Italy. In the last ten years, nearly 1.5 million people have arrived, often from poor nations of Africa (Senegal, Ethiopia, Somalia, Tunisia, and Morocco) and Asia (the Philippines and China).

Most of these immigrants enter the "hidden" economy in Italy, working illegally for low wages in industry, agriculture, and the service sector. For example, African immigrants now harvest the tomatoes in the South and work as street vendors, selling souvenirs and goods to Italians and tourists alike. Philippine immigrants labor as domestic helpers, and the Chinese have opened restaurants in many cities. Some immigrants, arriving illegally, drift into criminal activities, often those dominated by organized crime in the South.

Recreation

The most popular sport in Italy is soccer. Italians, particularly Italian men, love their Sunday "football." In 1982 Italy won the quadrennial World Cup soccer championship, played in Spain. Within minutes of the Italians' victory over West Germany, the streets and piazzas of all Italy—large cities and tiny villages—filled with people in joyous celebration: The Italian national team was the best in the world. The Italians' enthusiasm was such that they even damaged many valuable monuments.

Italy hosted the World Cup matches in June and July of 1990. The Italian national team—called the *Azzurri* (the Blues)—was a strong entry and won third place. The Italians supported their team enthusiastically: Most of the country stayed at home in front of the television when their team played.

The daily newspaper with the largest circulation is not a political paper, but rather the pink-colored daily *Gazzetta dello Sport* (the *Sports Gazette*). It carries the latest results of the soccer games, the gossip about players, and the standings of each team in Italy's three leagues. In addition to the professional teams, Italy has hundreds of village teams that play against each other weekly, carrying on rivalries whose origins often lie several hundred years in the past.

Basketball is also a popular sport in Italy. There are two semiprofes-

Soccer (called calcio) *is the most popular sport in Italy, played professionally and in pickup games such as this one in a Florence* piazza.

sional leagues with a total of thirty-three teams. And some of the most famous basketball players in Italy are not even Italian: They are Americans who play under contract for a number of years in the Italian leagues. Basketball is, however, the only American sport that has caught on in Italy; few Italians play and far fewer follow either baseball or football.

Racing of all sorts is also quite popular in modern Italy. The greatest passion is reserved for bicycle racing, a sport in which Italians have always done quite well. Each spring the Tour of Italy draws national attention and live television coverage for most of the two weeks that it takes for the world's top bicyclists to race around Italy.

Both car and motorcycle racing have fans in Italy as well. Formula-1 high-speed automobile racing is followed by several million Italians

Another very popular sport is bicycle racing. The Tour of Italy in the spring attracts the top riders in the world. Here, the racers pass by Milan's main cathedral.   Leo de Wys, Inc./Marka

each year. Two of the world's top drivers are Italians, and the Ferrari automobile factory turns out some of the world's best racing cars. The attention of the Formula-1 fans throughout the world focuses on Italy and the racetrack in the Romagna town of Imola during the summer's Grand Prix.

Hunting is another common sporting activity, but it is one that has created much controversy in the last few years. Three or four thousand years of continuous human civilization have left little wildlife in Italy, and intensive hunting of the few birds and animals that remain has reduced numbers even further. Urban development, industrial growth, and environmental pollution have also taken their toll. Popular referendums to eliminate hunting have been put forward on a number of occasions. The minority in favor of hunting has so far been able to defeat these motions.

Passeggiata

Perhaps the most popular form of recreation for Italians is simply walking. The old tradition of a Sunday *passeggiata*—a walk around town—still lives on, even in the large cities like Rome and Milan. In the smaller towns and villages of Italy, almost all the population fills the streets for a few hours each Sunday afternoon after lunch, the main meal of the day.

Italians are also avid hikers, and well-constructed and clearly marked trails cover the Apennines and the Alps. Mountain climbing is also a popular sport, particularly in the north of Italy. Most Italians, though, are content to walk leisurely through the woods for their recreation. Some people go to the countryside and forests in search of wild mushrooms to harvest and eat later. The most determined collectors have their own secret areas where they go for their *funghi* several times a year. Even if it's only for a few hours, the weekend walk remains a

An antihunting demonstration. A woman dressed as a rabbit takes up a rifle to defend the rights of animals. A referendum to eliminate hunting in Italy was defeated in 1990, but the issue remains an important one for Italy's environmentalists. Agenzia Fotogiornalistica Cronaca Nuova/Carlo Bozzardi

Bocce, *akin to bowling, is still a very popular pastime in Italy. The interest can be seen in the concentration on the faces of both players and spectators.* Agenzia Fotogiornalistica Cronaca Nuova/Carlo Bozzardi

way for Italians to enjoy their land, which until recently was the foundation of the Italian peasant culture.

Most Italians dedicate August to their yearly vacation. Nearly all of Italy is on holiday for at least two weeks in that month. The larger cities empty as people head to the sea and the mountains; restaurants and stores close and the factories shut down. The most popular vacation spots remain the beaches, where resort areas fill to overflowing. The number of Italians who travel abroad for their holidays has doubled recently, but four out of five still prefer to vacation in Italy.

The Southern Question

The great range of geography and climate in Italy make it a nation of many different regions. The history of each area differs as well, increasing the distinctiveness of the regions. One result is that even today, more than one hundred years after unification, most Italians identify with their local areas, rather than with the nation. This attitude is called *campanelismo*, or loyalty to the clock tower in the village square. "Being Italian" is still an abstract concept; the differences among the many regions are still too many and too great for a single label like "Italy."

The most important of these regional variations is the difference between northern and southern Italy. The Italian South is poorer than the North. The debate about why this is so focuses on something called the "Southern Question."

South?

Where does the South begin? The answer depends on where you are in Italy when you ask this question. For the Romans, the South starts just around Naples. For the Florentines, the South begins at Rome. For the people of Bologna or Milan, the Italian South includes all the land from Florence to the southern tip of the peninsula. Few Italians wish to think of themselves as "southerners." This form of prejudice is part of the Southern Question.

The South can be defined geographically. Its northern border lies in the Campania region, around the city of Naples, and the coastal region called the Molise. The South then extends down the peninsula through Puglia, Calabria, and Basilicata, and then across the straits to the island of Sicily. Sardinia, Italy's other large island in the Tyrrhennian Sea, is also part of southern Italy. This definition of the South takes in about one third of Italy's total land area and nearly 35 percent of its population.

The origins of the problems facing the South lie in the combination of a harsh climate and difficult geography. Much closer to Africa than to Europe, southern Italy and the two large islands of Sicily and Sardinia have historically been very difficult lands on which to live. Agriculture still suffers from uncertain rainfall. The soil is poor. The vast extent of mountains limits the amount of land available for agriculture. The South has always been a poor land.

Those who governed Italy have neglected the South. Until recently, little attention was given to helping southern peasants improve their lives. Before the unification of Italy, owners of large amounts of southern land (who frequently did not live in the South themselves) took whatever profits they gained from agriculture and used these to support a luxurious life in the cities, far away from the misery of the peasants in the fields.

Shepherding remains a common occupation in the rural areas of Italy, especially in the South and on the islands of Sardinia and Sicily. A man with a young sheep keeps a close eye on his flock near Palma de Montechiaro, Sicily. Thomas Roma

This situation did not change when the South was incorporated into the new Kingdom of Italy in 1861. The new leaders of Italy, mostly northern men from the region of Piedmont, demonstrated the same lack of interest in the South. Southern Italians occasionally turned to banditry as a way of life in these difficult conditions. The result was even harsher treatment—much of Sicily was put under the rule of the army during the 1860's and 1870's to deal with the bandits.

Misery and poverty continued in the South through the first half of the twentieth century. The only solution was emigration. Hundreds of thousands of Italians left Calabria and Sicily between 1890 and 1910, seeking a better life elsewhere in Europe and even as far away as

Argentina, Brazil, Chile, Canada, and the United States. The situation for the South did not change under Mussolini. The Fascists found it just as easy to ignore the South and its problems as had earlier Italian governments.

A First Step

It was only after the Second World War that the Italian state began to concern itself seriously with the South. In the mid-1950's, the government initiated a massive program of investment in the South, designed to improve agriculture and lay the foundations for a more modern and prosperous society. A special fund, the *Cassa per il Mezzogiorno* (Fund for the South), was created. Great sums of money financed special projects in the South. Swamps were drained, and other land reclamation projects turned previously unusable land into productive farms. Irrigation projects brought water to formerly arid areas. Electricity arrived in isolated southern villages. The beginnings of a modern road network, including the extension of the Italian *autostrada* (freeway) into Calabria, connected the South to the rest of Italy and Europe.

All these projects provided substantial benefits to the South, though they represented only the beginnings of a long process of bringing it up to northern levels. The original problems of poor soil and harsh climate continue to limit the productivity of southern agriculture even today.

Cathedrals in the Desert In the 1960's, the *Cassa* tackled a second major problem facing the South: the lack of industry. Several trillion lire was invested in the construction of the first large-scale factories in the South. But the *Cassa*'s initiative lacked overall planning and the results were often disappointing. Huge factories were built on some of the best land, damaging agriculture in the South. The factories

North and South by the Numbers

Northern and southern Italy are different in so many ways that they are often considered two separate countries. The following figures give an idea of some of the differences between North and South (1989 figures).

	North	South	All Italy
Population	64.4%	35.6%	
Men	48.4%	49.1%	48.6%
Women	51.6%	50.9%	51.4%
Children under age 14	19%	26%	22%
Adults over age 65	14%	11%	13%
Working Population			
(% of total pop.)	44.0%	38.5%	42.0%
Employed in agriculture	6.6%	15.3%	9.3%
Employed in industry	36.0%	23.3%	32.1%
Other activities	57.4%	61.4%	58.6%
Women in labor force	38.4%	33.8%	36.9%
Unemployment	7.4%	21.1%	12.0%
Average per Capita Income			
(1988)	$15,500	$8,900	$13,000
Family			
Family size	2.9	3.3	3.0
Birthrate			
(per 10,000 people)	82	128	99
Marriages			
(per 10,000 people)	51	62	55
Divorce			
(per 10,000 people)	6.8	3.0	5.4
Divorce			
(as percent of marriages)	13.3%	4.6%	9.7%

Infant mortality rate; (1988; percent of live births)	0.8%	1.1%	0.9%
Education (% of total population)			
Illiteracy rate	1.4%	6.3%	3.1%
High school graduates	16.7%	14.0%	15.8%
University graduates	2.9%	2.6%	2.8%
Church and State (% of all marriages)			
Religious ceremony	80.6%	88.1%	83.7%
Civil ceremony only	19.4%	11.9%	16.3%
Election Results (1987; % of total vote)			
Christian Democracy	31.7%	39.7%	34.3%
Italian Communist Party	28.5%	22.5%	26.6%
Business size (% of all businesses)			
Fewer than 2 employees	18.5%	31.3%	20.9%
More than 1,000 employees	16.2%	7.0%	14.4%
Towns with population over 100,000	33	17	50
Services			
Telephones (per 1,000 people)	597	358	509
Televisions (per 1,000 people)	288	199	256
Automobiles (per 1,000 people)	482	322	424
Daily newspapers (total number)	92	18	110
Government spending on theater/sports (yearly, per person, $1=1,300 lire)	$48	$20	$37

From: ISTAT, *Le Regioni in Cifre*, edizione 1990; ISTAT, *Annuario Statistico Italiano*, 1989.

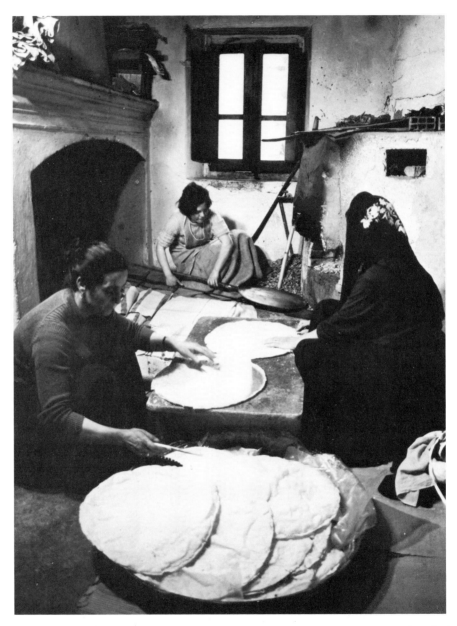

Women in Sardinia making bread at home in the 1960's. This very thin bread, called carta musica ("sheet music"), is baked in a wood oven. Very little has changed in this process over the past hundred years. ENIT, Roma

often stood alone, far away from the cities and necessary services. Many of these factories never operated at a profit. They became "cathedrals in the desert"—splendid but isolated examples of industry brought to an area not yet ready for it.

There were other problems with the development of the South as well. Much of the money spent in southern Italy was allocated according to political favors. Scandals and illegal use of state funds were common. Organized crime often controlled the state-financed construction projects, bringing greater wealth and power to those people involved in illegal activities in the South.

Today, southern Italy is better off than it has ever been. The dry and sunny climate of the South plus the hundreds of miles of beautiful coastline have contributed to a boom in summer tourism, which is now southern Italy's most important economic activity. However, in virtually every social and economic category, the comparison between North and South shows southern Italy to be a traditional, relatively backward and disadvantaged region.

Italy has still not found the answer to the Southern Question. The problems of climate and geography are not easily overcome by state programs. The damage caused by centuries of neglect cannot be canceled in a short period. The prejudice that much of northern Italy shows against the southerners may take several generations to erase. Though things are improving in southern Italy, the problem of an economically and culturally poorer South will remain in Italy for some time to come.

The Mafia

Another important aspect of the Southern Question is organized crime. The term "Mafia" is most often used to refer to crime in the South. But "Mafia" is a misleading label for two reasons. First, no single criminal organization is active in all areas of the South. The specific term describes only the criminal activities of many different groups on the island of Sicily, though it has also become the overall label for the problem of organized crime throughout Italy. In the region around Naples, crime is connected to groups called the *Camorra*; in Calabria, organized crime is called the *'Ndranghita* (a word that blends both local dialect and ancient Greek). Various areas in Italy give their own names to illegal activities: even in crime, Italy's regionalism is apparent.

It is also a mistake to think that there is a single individual directing the activities of any one of these three regional groups. There is no "godfather" in control. Crime in southern Italy is divided among many different families, each dominating its own area. These families compete with each other as they attempt to increase the territories they control. Again, even in illegal activities, crime reflects another important Italian tradition: the importance of the family.

Vendetta   Organized crime has a long history in the southern regions of Italy. The Sicilian Mafia, for example, started long before Italy was created as a single nation in the 1860's. The first *mafiosi* were probably bandits, living off robbery in the more isolated areas of Sicily. But after Italian unification, the Mafia grew, spreading throughout the island in the absence of a strong state.

When the Italian government showed little interest in regulating Sicilian agriculture, the Mafia stepped in. It drew up contracts that brought growers and distributors together, it set the price of citrus fruits and other crops, and the Mafia ensured that both parties respected the terms of these contracts. The Mafia also guaranteed farmers access to water, a crucial resource in arid Sicily. The crime families established wages for peasants and made certain that owners would not face a rebellious work force. Those who did not respect the terms of these agreements, or who informed on criminal activities, were often murdered—the *vendetta*. The Sicilian Mafia charged for all these services: This was the source of its profit. Had the Italian state shown a real interest in the South, the Mafia would not have been able to occupy this position regulating the southern economy.

The Sicilian Mafia and the *Camorra* of the Naples area also made money from many other sources, including gambling, prostitution, smuggling of all sorts of goods (like cigarettes), and offering protection for legitimate businesses in the South.

Things changed for organized crime in the 1950's. Development projects aimed at improving the South provided new opportunities. Larger profits were available by using the state funds of the *Cassa per il Mezzogiorno* for construction. The freeway system in the South and public-housing projects both served to enrich the crime families. Political contacts guaranteed access to state money: in exchange for preferred treatment in the awarding of contracts, the Mafia and *Camorra* offered votes. Many southern politicians in the Christian Democracy accepted this tradeoff.

Drugs and Other New Crime

Organized crime has expanded into a new activity in the last few decades: trade in illegal drugs. The amount of money to be made in drug smuggling, particularly heroin, is enormous. The yearly profits from drug sales make the organized crime families of the Sicilian Mafia one of the wealthiest business organizations in the world.

The heroin trade has changed the nature of organized crime in the South in many ways. First, by making the Mafia and *Camorra* richer, drugs have made the crime families more powerful. The money recycled from drugs is deposited in banks and invested in legitimate business activities throughout Italy, Europe, and the world.

The drug trade has also made the Mafia groups much more violent.

The Mafia, *Camorra*, and *'Ndranghita* now have some of the best-armed private armies in the world. Wars between the crime families have escalated enormously. Crime-related murder is increasingly common in Sicily, Campania, and Calabria. Organized crime has also moved into trade in illegal weapons. All these aspects of the "new" Mafia make organized crime the most serious threat to law and order in modern Italy.

The *'Ndranghita* has recently specialized in kidnapping. Since the late 1970's, Calabrian crime families have kidnapped over sixty people, most often the sons or daughters of wealthy northern businessmen. These young people have been held captive in the rugged mountain area of Calabria called the Aspromonte until their families have paid ransoms. The longest kidnapping, that of a sixteen-year-old, lasted nearly two and a half years. The Italian state has failed to deal with these crimes. Only a small number of the kidnappings have been solved by the police, and few people have been convicted.

Omertà   Dealing with organized crime in the South is an extremely difficult problem. A code of silence, called the *omertà*, is rarely broken, ensuring that criminal activities are not revealed to the police. Over the past years, however, some individuals from within the Mafia, the *Camorra*, and the *'Ndranghita* have revealed the names of the leaders of many crime families, making criminal prosecution possible. The Italian state has also taken the first steps toward a possible solution to the problem of organized crime. Judges and lawyers who specialize in Mafia-related affairs now pool resources for more effective legal action. These judges have shown much courage in bringing charges. New laws allow the courts greater access to financial records, allowing investigators to trace illegal money back to its source. Special police units trained to deal with the Mafia, *Camorra*, and *'Ndranghita* have been stationed in the South. International cooperation among law

One solution to the Mafia's involvement in drug traffic is to take the profit out of the business by decriminalizing the drugs. The "antiprohibitionists" support this idea.
Agenzia Fotogiornalistica Cronaca Nuova/Carlo Bozzardi

enforcement agencies, especially between Italy and the United States on drug-related crimes, is working better than it ever has.

Perhaps the most important part of the fight against crime in the South is the attitude of the southerners themselves. Organized crime can be defeated only when it is rejected by the people. A generation of young southern Italians have shown their determination to free their regions of organized crime in many recent demonstrations. A changed outlook toward the Mafia, the *Camorra*, and the *'Ndranghita* is needed before better police and legal action can effectively tackle the problems of crime in the South. Today, however, the Mafia remains one of the most serious problems facing Italy.

Church and State

Rome is not only the capital of Italy. It is also the city of the pope, the spiritual and administrative center of Catholicism, the most popular Christian faith in the world. The Vatican, headquarters of the Catholic Church, lies only a short distance across the Tiber River from Italy's national parliament.

Church and state have coexisted in Italy for centuries, and the Catholic Church continues to be very important in contemporary Italy. Relations between the Church and the modern Italian state was one of the important issues facing the nation after the Second World War. Wishing to avoid a dispute over religion, the Italian Parliament incorporated the Lateran Pacts, signed in 1929 between the Fascist leader Mussolini and Pope Pius XI, into the constitution of the Republic of Italy in 1948 without major changes other than the elimination of Catholicism as the official religion of the country.

Only in 1984 did the Church and state substantially modify the Lateran Pacts. A Socialist Prime Minister (Bettino Craxi) and a Polish Pope (John Paul II) agreed to revise certain aspects of the earlier agreement and sign a new concordat. The Church's bank was brought under the jurisdiction of Italian financial laws (following a spectacular Vatican banking scandal earlier in the 1980's). The 1984 revision also established new criteria for religious marriages and made religious education in state schools voluntary.

A Catholic Italy?

The acceptance of the new concordat by the Vatican was a sign of the declining influence of the Church in an increasingly secular society. Is Italy still a Catholic country? How Catholic are the Italians? These are both difficult questions to answer.

Most Italians certainly consider themselves Catholic. The great majority are baptized in the Church, most are married in religious ceremonies, and many are buried with a Church funeral. Most Italians attend Sunday Mass at least twice a year, on the most important religious holidays of Easter and Christmas. But less than one quarter of them attend Sunday services on a regular basis.

The clearest proof of how much influence the Church has lost in Italy came in recent votes on social legislation. Divorce became legal in Italy only at the end of 1970. Four years later, the Vatican sponsored a referendum to cancel the divorce law. The Italian people disregarded the strong recommendations of both the Pope and the Christian Democracy and voted to keep divorce. In 1981, a second vote sponsored by the Vatican aimed at canceling a liberal abortion law passed by the Italian Parliament a few years earlier. Again the Italians, this time two thirds of them, voted to keep abortion legal in Italy. These were two major defeats for the Church on issues that the Vatican considered very important. The Church now has a more limited role in the social questions of modern Italy, and most Italians increasingly accept Church authority only in religious issues.

A Catholic youth movement called Communion and Liberation is an important exception to this picture of declining Church influence in Italian society. The Communion and Liberation group is dedicated to reestablishing a Catholic moral vision in Italy. Some of its followers seek election to the Chamber of Deputies and Senate as candidates of the Christian Democracy. Most of the movement's members are under twenty-five years old. They are especially active in the Italian universities. Communion and Liberation is still a small movement (with perhaps 100,000 members) and is largely restricted to the North. The movement enjoys the support of Pope John Paul II and some of the leading Christian Democracy politicians.

The Church and the Pope

The Vatican City includes the land surrounding St. Peter's Church and three other churches in Rome. It is a small country (about 100 acres, just over one sixth of a square mile or two fifths of a square kilometer) with a permanent population of only one thousand. The Vatican City has its own bank, railroad station, flag, television channel, radio station, postal system (the most efficient in Italy), and a daily newspaper (*L'Osservatore Romano—The Roman Observer*). The Vatican also has a police force, ceremonial troops for the pope called the Swiss Guards.

The main church is named for the first Bishop of Rome, Peter, who may have been crucified by the Roman Emperor Nero in A.D. 67. A shrine was built on Peter's burial site in the middle of the second century; work started on a real church in 315. The current St. Peter's Church dates from the early 1500's. Monumental in scale, St. Peter's dwarfs all other Catholic churches in the world except for an even larger replica of the Roman church being built in the African nation of the Ivory Coast. A grand, open square stands in front of St. Peter's. This piazza, an architectural masterpiece designed by Bernini in the mid-1600's, is where thousands gather on holy days awaiting papal blessings and pronouncements. Alongside St. Peter's stands the Vatican Palace, begun in the eighth century and completed in the sixteenth, which is one of the largest buildings in the world.

Within St. Peter's Church and the adjoining Vatican Museum are some of the greatest masterpieces of western art. These include Michelangelo's statue of the *Pietà* and his frescoes in the Sistine Chapel. Hundreds of other paintings and statues also fill the Vatican Museum. There are thousands of cultural artifacts from societies all over the world, brought back to Rome by Catholic missionaries. The

*Catholics from all over the world gather each Sunday in St. Peter's Square to hear the Pope's sermon and receive his blessing. This is the holiday of Pentecost in 1991. L'Osservatore Romano/*Arturo Mari

Vatican's archives chronicle the history of the Church and Europe over the past two thousand years. Hundreds of researchers work among these priceless documents. St. Peter's Church and the Vatican Museum are among the great cultural treasures of the world.

Originally, the pope was only the bishop of the Church in Rome. That role gradually expanded over the centuries, and now he is the highest authority of world Roman Catholicism. The pope is the spiritual leader of the Church, and Catholics everywhere look to him for religious inspiration and moral example in their lives.

The pope also stands at the top of a pyramid of power. In theory, he has all executive, legislative, and judicial powers. In reality, the pope is the top administrator of the affairs of the Church. The Vatican has a secretary of state, a diplomatic corps, and a council of bishops.

The pope, who must be male, is an elected leader who serves for life. He is chosen by the College of Cardinals, an advisory body of the highest Church officials. The cardinals have the responsibility of seeing to the overall well-being of the Church throughout the world. Upon the death of a pope, the College of Cardinals meets in secret session in the Sistine Chapel to select a new Church leader.

The election of a new pope is a moment of great excitement and tension within the Church. Catholics the world over follow the election closely because the choice of a new leader is also a choice of direction for the Church. Enormous crowds gather in St. Peter's Square to await the results of the cardinals' meeting. A small stove is used to pass a smoke signal from the Sistine Chapel to the outside world. Black smoke means that the cardinals have not yet chosen a new leader for the Church; white smoke indicates the election of a new pope, who soon afterward greets the crowds from the central balcony of St. Peter's.

The pope takes on an official name upon election. The current pope (since 1978) is John Paul II, although his real name is Karol Wojtyla. John Paul II comes from Poland, and he is the first non-Italian pope in

Order of Malta

The world's smallest country is closely tied to the Vatican. This is the Sovereign Military Order of Malta, located in a single building on an elegant shopping street in the center of Rome. The Order of Malta, in the Malta Palace, may be the only country to have a street address: 68 via Condotti.

The Sovereign Military Order of Malta is a nation without citizens but with a worldwide membership of nearly ten thousand instead. Its leader, called the Prince Grand Master, is appointed by the pope. The Order was founded in 1048 to provide aid for Christian pilgrims traveling from Europe to the Holy Lands. The Order's principal activity today remains that of administering hospitals and providing medical care in many areas of the world.

over 450 years. John Paul II has promoted an active role for the Church in modern politics, especially in the Third World and in Eastern Europe. He is also a traveling pope, who visited nearly one hundred countries and logged more than 150,000 miles in the first ten years of his papacy.

Earlier this century, another pope, John XXIII, was one of the most popular leaders in the history of the Catholic Church. John XXIII, an Italian, was Pope from 1958 to 1963. He was the first pope to travel outside Rome and its immediate confines in nearly one hundred years, bringing the Church directly to Italians elsewhere on the peninsula. John XXIII also initiated a great reform movement within the Church: the Second Vatican Council. This council worked for three years to modernize the Church and change the Vatican's structure. John XXIII first opened the Vatican toward both the Third World and toward the Soviet Union. He also eliminated Latin as the language of the Church Mass, allowing Catholics to celebrate their faith in their own native tongues. Many Catholics today still remember John XXIII as the Pope of reform, who did a great deal to move the Church closer to its followers.

Other Religions in Italy

Catholicism is not the only religion in Italy. There are many other Christian denominations and sects, including Russian Orthodox, a Mormon missionary community, Jehovah's Witnesses, Seventh-Day Adventists, and followers of the Assembly of God. All of these, however, are rather small groups. More important is the larger Protestant community in Italy, which includes Lutherans, Baptists, Methodists, and Anglicans, and totals approximately 75,000 people.

There are also around 40,000 Jews in Italy today. The Roman synagogue is the center of Italian Jewry. Many other cities also have Jewish communities. Venice and Ferrara, both in the North, have the largest.

Jews have been in Italy since the ancient days of the Roman Empire. They were among some of the earliest settlers along the Tiber River. Until two hundred years ago, Italian Jews were persecuted and allowed to live only in certain neighborhoods. These areas were called the *ghettos*, and the Jewish neighborhood of Venice was one of the first ghettos in Europe. Discrimination was especially common in the lands controlled by the popes, where Jews were granted few civil rights and prohibited from marrying Catholics.

Reform began under Napoleon, who granted Jews equal status and citizenship in the areas of Italy controlled by France. Later, Italian Jews played important roles in the uprisings of the *Risorgimento* period; some were among Garibaldi's *Mille* in the wars in the South, and a few fought to conquer Rome for the Kingdom of Italy in 1870.

Religions overlap and mix in Italy. In the midst of Rome's Jewish ghetto, a Catholic church has been built inside the remains of a Roman temple. Next door stands a restaurant specializing in Jewish cuisine.

Italian Jews were elected to the first parliament of Italy in 1861; the first Jewish prime minister was appointed in 1910.

The lack of discrimination against the Jews was true even for most of the years of Fascism. Some Jews supported Mussolini when he came to power, and many enrolled in the Italian Fascist Party. Harsh racial laws, passed in 1937, remained largely unenforced until Italy's entry into the the Second World War in 1940. Italy was a Fascist nation and an ally of Nazi Germany, but that did not prevent Italians from helping their Jewish neighbors hide or escape even after the German occupation in 1943.

Modern Italy is one of the few European countries in which there is little anti-Semitism. Since the creation of a unified nation, the history of the Jews in Italy has been one of integration, not separation. Jews are active in all areas of Italian society, politics, the educational system, the military and the economy. Jews are so thoroughly assimilated in Italy that foods from the Jewish community (such as fried artichokes and cod fillets) have become traditional dishes in some of the country's regions.

An Islamic religious community has appeared in Italy over the past several years. The first presence of Arabs in Italy dates back to the 700's when they conquered the island of Sicily. Their influence may still be seen in some of the architecture and the mosques of Palermo. The current Arab population, now estimated at around 85,000, is made up of immigrants searching for work and a better standard of living. They have brought the Islamic faith back again to Italy. The largest mosque outside the Arab world is under construction in Rome and will serve as a gathering point for the Muslims of Italy and Europe when completed in 1992. Modern Italy has been generally quite tolerant toward other religions in the country. The newly arrived followers of Islam can expect to integrate smoothly and add another element to the increasingly diverse religious picture of Italy.

Culture:
The Arts, Sciences,
and Education

The importance of centuries of history in Italy is seen in the country's arts and sciences. The traditions of ancient Rome and the Renaissance are often present in the minds of modern Italian artists and intellectuals.

Arts

Contemporary Italian art actually suffers under the weight of its own history. The splendors of ancient Rome and the golden age of the Renaissance focus more attention on the paintings and sculpture of the past than on the art of the present. Only a short-lived movement called Futurism, which flourished immediately before the First World War, saw Italy at the forefront of innovative, modern art.

Restoration and its Problems

Most restoration work involves the removal of the dirt and grime of the centuries from sculptures, paintings, and buildings. This is a very delicate cleaning job, which has to be done carefully so as not to damage the underlying art.

Restoration can also involve questions of the art itself, as the cleaning of Michelangelo's fresco paintings in the Vatican's Sistine Chapel in Rome reveals.

Painted by Michelangelo between 1508 and 1512, the frescoes on the ceiling are among the masterpieces of Western art. The goal of the restoration project, begun in 1980, was to return the works to their original appearance. It took over four billion lire ($4 million) and ten years to clean the frescoes on the chapel's ceiling. The chemicals used brought to the surface bright and vibrant colors that had long been hidden underneath centuries of smoke and dust. The result was a controversy. Few experts could agree on whether those were the original colors Michelangelo had used. Some others protested the very idea of the restoration itself, arguing that it was better to let the art age naturally and learn to accept the duller colors and layers of smoke.

Disagreements about the restoration will continue. The second phase of the project, the restoration of the *Last Judgement* frescoes (painted by Michelangelo between 1535 and 1541), began in 1990 and will undoubtedly create more arguments.

Pope Paul III commissioned Michelangelo to decorate a wall of the Sistine Chapel in the 1530's. In one section of The Last Judgement, *St. Bartholomew holds his skin after being flayed alive. Michelangelo put his own face on the skin of the martyred saint.* Italian Cultural Institute

Somewhat overwhelmed by the past, the arts in modern Italy have taken other forms. Much attention is given to the preservation and restoration of the older art treasures. The Italians have developed some of the most sophisticated techniques for protecting ancient art, and specialists the world over come to Italy to perfect their craft.

The ancient arts for which Italy is quite famous face serious problems of maintenance and conservation. Restoration of art and buildings, guards for museums and archaeological sites, and guides to provide information for the visitors are all quite expensive. The Italian state has shown itself unwilling to devote much government money to these projects. It stands to reason that Italy by itself should not have to take care of a cultural heritage that really belongs to all of Europe.

Literature

Italian literature is deeply influenced by older traditions. Italy's past contribution to Western literature is enormous. The Medieval and Renaissance writers created a rich literary legacy for Italy. *Risorgimento* authors such as Alessandro Manzoni (1775–1873) reinforced this tradition of fine writing.

Some of the most important modern novelists were deeply influenced by Fascism and the Second World War. Authors such as Carlo Levi (1902–1975), Primo Levi (1919–1987), Curzio Malaparte (1898–1957), Elsa Morante (1912–   ), Cesare Pavese (1908–1950), and Ignazio Silone (1900–1978) wrote about the political and social problems of dictatorship and war. Their works reflect a need to understand these experiences and a desire to discuss the real problems facing Italy. (Some of the titles by recent Italian writers that are available in English are listed in the Bibliography.)

One of the most creative of modern Italian writers was Italo Calvino

(1923–1985). Calvino's interest in folktales and fables led him increasingly into a semifantasy world where humans and their emotions are still important. Another contemporary writer of great fame was Alberto Moravia (1907–1990), who was also a respected literary and social critic.

Luigi Pirandello (1867–1937) is one of the dominant figures in twentieth-century Italian literature. His novels focus on the theme of the individual's identity within modern society. Pirandello also wrote for the theater, keeping to his favorite theme of the fragility of identity in the contemporary world. Pirandello's best-known work is *Six Characters in Search of an Author* (1921).

The Italian theater continues to produce master playwrights. One of the foremost contemporary authors in this field is Dario Fo. Fo combines the art of the clown with modern satire to produce political theater that makes one laugh and cry at the same time. His most famous plays include *Comic Mystery* (1969), *Accidental Death of an Anarchist* (1970,) and *Can't Pay! Won't Pay!* (1974).

Two philosophers dominate the Italian intellectual tradition. The writings of Benedetto Croce (1866–1952) on aesthetics, history, politics, and ethics have influenced three generations of Italians. Antonio Gramsci (1891–1937), imprisoned by the Fascists for his opposition to Mussolini, theorized about culture, society, and politics in new ways that have influenced intellectuals throughout the world.

Opera

Italians made enormous contributions to modern culture in opera and orchestral music. The word *opera* is Italian, which has come to mean "work in music." It is an art form combining a text (called a libretto) with music (singers and orchestra) and often dance. The first opera was an Italian production dating from the sixteenth century. The grand music and often intricate stories remain immensely popular. Italians still sing passages from some of the more famous operas while going about their daily work. La Scala, in Milan, is one of the most famous opera houses in the world, though the theater in Venice, built in 1637, is thought to be the oldest opera house.

Many of the world's greatest operas are the works of Italians. Giuseppe Verdi (1813–1901) is perhaps the most famous. His works

Giuseppe Verdi (1813–1901) was Italy's most famous and prolific composer of opera. This portrait is by Giovanni Boldini.   The Bettmann Archive

include *Rigoletto*, *Aïda*, *La Traviata*, *Il Trovatore*, and *Otello*, all of which are standard offerings in the season of many great opera companies. Giacomo Puccini (1858–1924) was another great Italian composer. His best known operas are *La Bohème*, *Tosca*, *Madama Butterfly*, and *Turandot*. Other well-known Italian operas include *The Barber of Seville* and *William Tell*, both by Gioacchino Rossini (1792–1868), and *Don Pasquale* by Gaetano Donizetti (1797–1848).

Opera employs orchestral music, and the use of different instruments in this fashion was an Italian creation, dating from the 1590's in Venice. The first appearance of an orchestra, with forty instruments, took place in 1607, when the composer and director Claudio Monteverdi staged the opera *The Fable of Orpheus*. The use of orchestras without singers developed, and in the early eighteenth century, Antonio Vivaldi (1675–1741) composed two of his most famous works for orchestra, *The Four Seasons* and *Estro Armonico*. One of the world's legendary conductors was Arturo Toscanini (1867–1957), whose career included both La Scala in Milan and the Metropolitan Opera in New York. Claudio Abbado and others continue the Italian tradition of great conductors today.

The importance of opera in Italian culture has encouraged the appearance of great singers. Four of this century's leading opera stars are Italian: the tenors Enrico Caruso (1873–1921), Beniamino Gigli (1890–1957), and Luciano Pavarotti (1935–   ), and the soprano Katia Ricciarelli (1948–   ). Another great soprano, Maria Callas (1923–1977), was an American of Greek ancestry who spent much time in her adopted country, Italy.

Cinema

The movies is another art form in which Italians have excelled. Cinema was the most popular form of mass entertainment through the first half of the twentieth century. Though its origins lay in the 1890's, the cinema in Italy developed in the 1920's and 1930's. Under Mussolini, the Fascists created a national cinema institute and trained a generation of directors.

When the Second World War ended in 1945, Italian filmmakers were freed from the restrictions imposed by the Fascist government. They began to produce movies about real Italy: the devastation of the war (*Rome–Open City*), the difficulties of reconstruction (*The Bicycle Thief*), the poverty of their country and the peasants' world (*Bitter Rice*). The actors were often people taken from the streets. For nearly a decade, until the mid-1950's, Italian cinema produced scores of movies whose subject was daily life. This was the neorealist period of Italian cinema. Some of the most famous directors included Roberto Rossellini, Vittorio De Sica, and Luchino Visconti. Their films set a standard for two generations, and neorealism continues to influence Italian filmmaking today.

The economic boom of post-war Italy pushed the cinema in new directions. Comedies returned to Italian movie theaters. One of Italy's best-loved comics remains Totò, who made nearly one hundred films between 1945 and his death in 1967. Fascinated by the American West, Italian directors also made hundreds of "spaghetti westerns" in the post-war period. Sergio Leone was perhaps the best known of these directors.

In the late 1950's, Federico Fellini, one of Italy's greatest directors, began to make films that clearly broke with the traditions of neorealism. Fellini injected fantasy, dreams, and his own memories into his films. Fellini won two Oscars in the category of best foreign film: *The Nights of Cabiria* (1954) and *Amarcord* (1974). These Academy Awards were signs that the Italian cinema was recognized worldwide. Another director, Michelangelo Antonioni, made his mark with films such as *The Adventure*, which depicted the loneliness of modern life as

Italy lost the traditions of its peasant culture.

The 1950's and 1960's were a golden age for the movies in Italy. *Cinecittà* (Cinema City), outside Rome, became the Italian version of Hollywood. Great actors and actresses appeared, such as Anna Magnani, Sophia Loren, Vittorio Gassman, and Marcello Mastroianni. However, the 1980's saw the Italian film industry in the midst of a crisis. Only a few filmmakers (such as Lina Wertmüller and Nanni Moretti) continue to display the imagination and vision of their predecessors, and the number of moviegoers has fallen sharply. In 1990, Giuseppe Tornatore won another Oscar for his film, *Cinema Paradiso*. This may be the first signs of a recovery of the film industry in Italy.

Sciences

From the days of the early Renaissance, Italians have been active in the sciences. One field in which they have played a major role is physics. Guglielmo Marconi (1874–1937) was the inventor of the radio. Self-educated, and fascinated with electromagnetism from an early age, Marconi was the first to perfect the techniques for the transmission of sound over long distances through the air. Marconi won a Nobel Prize in physics in 1909 for his discoveries.

Another Italian, Enrico Fermi (1901–1954), broke new ground in theoretical physics. His research at the University of Rome in the 1920's led to the first ideas about the structure of the atom, and Fermi was awarded a Nobel Prize in 1938. In that same year, after Mussolini passed anti-Semitic laws, Fermi and his Jewish wife left Italy for the United States. In America, Fermi's contribution was decisive to the development of atomic energy, the construction of the first nuclear reactor (built in Chicago in 1942), and the theoretical work that lay behind the first atomic bomb.

The tradition of research in physics continues in Italy. Edoardo Amaldi (1908–   ) and Carlo Rubbia (1934–   ) are at the forefront of advanced research in this field. The testing laboratory for physics deep underneath Gran Sasso Mountain in central Italy is one of the world's finest.

In another scientific field, biology, one Italian woman stands out. Rita Levi-Montalcino (1909–   ) won a 1986 Nobel Prize in physiology for her work in neurobiology and research on the growth of nerve cells.

Schools

The Italian educational system is divided into five levels. The majority of schools are administered by the state, but there are many private schools (including a few universities) in Italy, some of which are run by the Catholic Church.

For the youngest children, ages three to five, there is an optional preschool. Mandatory education for Italians begins at age six in the elementary school. This lasts for five years, until age eleven. The "lower" secondary school then follows. It lasts for three years, at the end of which the student (age fourteen) must pass a state examination. The lower secondary school marks the end of obligatory education, though a new reform of the school system may soon raise the mandatory age to sixteen years.

Higher secondary school education comes next, and lasts for five more years, from age fifteen to nineteen. Having passed the state examination, students may choose among three different kinds of higher secondary schools: the *liceo*, which offers an advanced general education most suited to those students certain about their interest in the university; the *magistero* school, which prepares students for a teaching career; or the institute, a more vocation-oriented school. At the end

Montessori Schools

Maria Montessori (1870–1952), an Italian teacher, created a revolution in education for young people. With degrees in both medicine and literature, Montessori taught at the University of Rome in the early twentieth century. There she developed a new theory of education that eventually acquired her name, the Montessori Method.

Montessori viewed education in a new way—as the job of the student. She believed that children, stimulated but also mystified by the outside environment, search from a very early age to understand the world around them. The teacher's duty is to aid students in their own discoveries and to act as a guide to the children's self-education.

This theory of education and the partnership between teacher and student it implies contrasted with the focus on discipline and authority common in most schools. Montessori's ideas, however, spread rapidly and her method of instruction is now found in private schools throughout the world.

of the five years, students take another state examination (both written and oral).

The courses offered in Italian higher secondary schools are demanding and the state examination is a difficult one. All three kinds of secondary schools offer a general education in the arts and sciences along with an intensive study of a specialized subject matter. Students who complete upper secondary school in Italy graduate with a diploma based on more work and more study than at an American high school. The diploma allows them to apply for entry into the university.

Young high school students take their protest against an inefficient school system to the streets. The girls' sign reads, "We're not asking for the moon, only for our rights."
Agenzia Fotogiornalistica Cronaca Nuova/Carlo Bozzardi

University   The Italian universities take students from age nineteen. Students choose a field of study (called a faculty) and prepare themselves for a series of examinations on subjects related to that field. They attend lectures and study on their own and in groups in preparation for these tests. The number of examinations varies depending on the faculty chosen, but there are generally between twenty and thirty tests. The course of study is established by each faculty, and the individual student sets his or her own pace; most complete their examinations in four years of full-time study. However, there is no limit on the number of years a student may take to complete a course of study.

After the examinations comes research. The Italian university stu-

High School Graduation

Graduation from one of the three branches of the upper secondary school (high school) in Italy requires a passing grade on a national examination. Here are a few examples of the questions facing students at that examination (called the *maturità*) in 1990.

1. "The permanent threat of war arises from the lack of trust between nations, their reciprocal fear of suffering an aggressive attack, and the recurrent problem of expansionist policies. For these reasons, today more than ever, it is necessary to create a state of trust and security among the peoples of the world that will remove the danger of war and assure the basic conditions for the maintenance of a stable peace." Reflect on this proposal, indicating if you see any signs favoring this much-desired universal peace on today's international scene. (For all students)

2. "Science is often accused of having brought terrible dangers to humanity by giving it excessive power over nature" (Konrad Lorenz). In your opinion, what arguments could be used to confirm or refute this accusation? (For students in the Scientific Schools and Technical Institutes)

dent must complete an in-depth research project in the chosen field of study. This usually requires a further six to twelve months of work. The results of this research are presented in a written thesis. A committee of professors evaluates the thesis and questions the student about its content and conclusions. The acceptance of the thesis marks the end of university study, and the student then graduates with a university diploma. This degree reflects greater knowledge at a higher level than a bachelor's degree from an American university.

Those interested in pursuing university study may continue with further research. After one or two years of additional work, the student receives a specialized degree, roughly the equivalent of an American doctorate.

Italian university education is open to anyone with a diploma from secondary school. There are no limits placed on the number of students who may enroll. The costs of university education are kept low so as not to exclude poorer students from attending the university. However, open access to higher education has created a serious problem: Italian universities are overcrowded and underfunded. Too many students overwhelm the university and its teaching staff. The quality of education often suffers as a result.

Protests

Student protests in Italy are common. In 1968 and again in 1977, students charged that higher education's focus on "great" works was too narrow and that university education did little to prepare students for the modern world. They also rejected the authoritarianism of many professors and administrators. Calling for free thinking and open expression of ideas in the university, the students demonstrated in most of the major cities of Italy. Their marches were quite often violently broken up by the police. But after a decade of protest, the students gained substantial reforms that went a long way toward creating a more modern and more liberal university.

Student protest appeared again in the universities in 1990. Marching under the banner of a black panther, the students condemned the lack of government funding and the poor quality of university services. Their nationwide protests gained much popular sympathy and many promises for improvement. However, few of the needed reforms have yet been enacted by the Parliament, and the Italian universities still struggle along under very difficult conditions.

Mixing high and popular cultures: Luciano Pavarotti, one of the world's greatest opera singers, stands with some of the top soccer players (Paolo Rossi and Pelé are in the front row) on the eve of the 1990 World Cup Soccer Championships held in Italy.
Agenzia Giornalistica Italia

Popular Culture

Alongside the "high" culture of the arts and sciences lies a flourishing "popular" culture in Italy. Here it is not the past but rather new and foreign influences that take the lead. Young Italians in particular are deeply affected by American attitudes and fashions. The fast food of hamburgers, french fries, and soft drinks, along with skateboards, American rock and roll, and discos are all part of the daily life of Italian teens.

The result is a rather striking generation gap. Italian grandparents, dressed formally, moving on foot or bicycle and still tied to the simpler way of life of a poorer, rural Italy, often live with grandchildren in jeans and T-shirts, who roar by on mopeds and listen to music on their

Television

The most powerful means of communication and the most popular form of entertainment today is certainly the television. Italy has both public and private television. There are three public channels, owned by the Italian state, which have exclusive rights to broadcast live throughout the nation. Politics enters even into the world of Italian television: the Christian Democrats, the Socialists, and the ex-Communists each control their own channel. Commercial advertising is strictly limited on the government channels, which are financed by government funds and a yearly tax on television sets.

There are also many private television channels, both national and local. Private TV is a business with commercials providing all of its income. The result is American-style television, spoken in the Italian language with many commercials. Soap operas (including *Dallas*, *The Young and the Restless*, and *Twin Peaks*) and cartoons (Walt Disney productions, *The Simpsons*) are dubbed into Italian. Copies of American game shows (like *The Price Is Right* and *The Newlywed Game*) are common.

Recently, the Italian Parliament passed legislation designed to protect the artistic quality of films on television by limiting the number of commercials the private channels could show during a movie. The owners of private television stations claimed that such restrictions would ruin their companies, but so far there have been no serious problems.

headphones. These two cultures, the older one with its centuries of traditions, and the newer one with its emphasis on youth and consumerism, could not be more different. Nonetheless, they coexist rather peacefully within many Italian families.

"At the Table": Daily Life and the Family

Though soccer is the national sport of Italy, it is not the real national pastime. That is food. The favorite activity of almost all Italians is eating. Food and all that accompanies it—the table, wine, conversation, and family—are the true passions of the Italian people. The best place to meet and get to know the Italians is at the table.

Bread and Wine

Italians love food, and Italy is famous for its regional cooking. Each area has its own popular dishes and specialities. Lombardy is known for its delicate rice dishes, Emilia for its rich sauces and stuffed pasta, and Tuscany for its soups and thick steaks. Naples is famous for its pizza and fish. Calabria has its spicy pasta, while the northern Alpine valleys have exquisite cheeses.

The many different Italys continue to eat quite different foods. Only in the past twenty years has a single national menu appeared, and that is largely due to the demands of foreign tourists who want to eat the same "spaghetti" in every restaurant in Italy. The Italians also eat their evening meal at different times. In the North, Italians sit down to their dinner table sometime before eight P.M., the Romans rarely eat before nine P.M., and in the South, especially during the hot summer, dinner may begin only after ten P.M.

Pasta   Despite the differences in cooking from region to region, pasta is the basic foundation for almost all Italian cooking. Pasta is the name given to a special, hard-grain wheat called *semolina*, which is mixed with water (and sometimes with eggs), formed into various shapes, added to salted boiling water, and cooked. Traditionally, Italian women prepared fresh pasta daily in the home. Spaghetti may be the best known pasta, but it is only one among many kinds. There are several other shapes of pasta.

Fresh pasta has been a part of the Italian diet for thousands of years. Dried pasta, however, arrived in Italy only as recently as the 1300's. Merchants from Genoa discovered this kind of pasta in the Arab world and brought it back to Italy. It took another four hundred years (until around 1700) for the tradition of cooking dried pasta to catch on in Italy. But once started, it spread quickly. By the early 1800's, cookbooks in Venice listed forty-eight different kinds of dried pasta.

Pasta is not the only staple at the base of the Italian way of eating. Rice and cornmeal (called *polenta*) are equally (or even more) important in certain northern and central areas of the country. Prior to the twentieth century, and in many areas until after the Second World War, Italian peasants ate little more than bread and beans.

Pasta is most commonly served with a sauce. The variety of different sauces in Italy is enormous. There are very simple ones based on butter and cheese; sauces with a few ingredients such as spicy pepperoni and garlic; the standard red tomato sauce; and finally, elaborate cheese and vegetable sauces that are actually stuffed inside the hollow sections of the larger shapes of pasta.

The most common sauce for pasta is made from tomatoes, but the tomato is a relatively new addition to the traditional Italian diet. Tomatoes came to Europe from Mexico and were unknown in Italy before the early 1500's when explorers first brought them back from the New World. At first the vegetable was thought to be poisonous and was used only as an ornamental plant. Sometime later, someone boiled the tomatoes down into a sauce and poured it on top of freshly cooked pasta. By the mid-1800's, a whole new way of eating was spreading from southern Italy northward.

Meals

Italians generally have one large and one smaller meal each day. The main meal begins with pasta or a soup. The pasta is served with one of several sauces, depending on the region, while the soup is commonly a vegetable or meat broth. The second plate is a meat or vegetable dish. More vegetables and often a salad will follow. At the end comes a dessert, fresh fruit, and sometimes cheese (there are more than 250 different types in Italy). Bread and wine are always present. Traditionally, the main meal in Italy was served at lunch, while dinner was substantially lighter. This pattern is changing, as more and more Italians do not have the time away from work to return home for a large lunch.

Breakfast hardly exists in Italy. Most people eat a sweet biscuit or a piece of toast and drink a cup of coffee before leaving home. Others simply stop at a local bar for a coffee or *cappuccino* (coffee with steamed milk) and a sweet roll before work. Coffee is a ritual in Italy.

At least twice a day, most Italians enjoy a concentrated coffee, called *espresso*, and take a short break from their regular duties. An *espresso* most often follows the evening meal as well.

A Healthy Diet

Up through the 1940's, the Italian diet was based on pasta, beans, vegetables, and bread. Cooking was done almost exclusively in olive oil. Poultry, pork, and beef rarely appeared: These were luxuries in peasant Italy, where meat was saved for special occasions and holiday meals. The traditional diet of Italy is now considered to be one of the healthiest in the world and is recommended by most experts in nutrition. However, the diet has changed for the worse over the past decades. Italians today eat much more meat than ever before. Doctors now encourage Italians to return to their older diet in the interests of better health.

A description of meals and diet does not convey the full meaning of food to the Italians. Food is also an important part of Italian culture. The main daily meal is the moment when the Italian family comes together to talk. The family lives and flourishes around the table. Over pasta, family members involve themselves deeply in each other's lives.

The importance of food is also an expression of an Italian attitude toward life. Italians take the most pleasure in the simple aspects of life. By focusing much attention on their food, the Italians concentrate on the richness and variety of life and the small details that make up each and every day. Food and contentment, food and happiness, food and life—these are all tied closely together in the Italian outlook.

Wine

The table is filled not only with food in the Italian household. Wine is always present at a meal. And wine is another of the other great passions of the Italians. Wine is thought of more as food than as an alcoholic beverage, and it is as important as the pasta, the vegetables, or the bread. Rarely do Italians drink a glass of wine by it-

Italians enjoy mixing with others. When the weather is good, the country's piazze are crowded until late at night. This is a midnight gathering near the Spanish Steps, a popular meeting place for young people in Rome, but the same scene could be found even in smaller provincial towns. Agenzia Fotogiornalistica Cronaca Nuova/Carlo Bozzardi

self, for wine accompanies food rather than standing alone. The country has no legal drinking age. Though Italians agree that young children should not drink, they cannot agree on how old "young" is.

There are hundreds of different types of wine in Italy. Again, each region has its own favorite. Most Italians drink their local wine with every meal. Either they buy the wine directly from peasant producers or they purchase it in large quantities from distributors. Because the common table wine of each region is the wine most people drink each day, this category accounts for most of the annual wine production in Italy. The very best of these regional wines are officially registered with the Italian government. Currently, there are over two hundred varieties whose quality is guaranteed by special labels.

Italians have been making wine for thousands of years. Centuries of experience have resulted in a choice of the best grape for each region of Italy, a grape that matches the soil and climate of the individual area. Good wine was the result of this good match. But wine making in Italy is now in the midst of major changes. Recently, Italian wineries have introduced new technologies imported from the United States. They have applied these techniques to the Italian tradition of fine wine grapes. The results have been spectacular, and the finest Italian wines are now recognized among the very best in the world.

Famous Italian Food

Italy is famous for a number of food specialities, which it exports throughout the world. Of its cheeses, the seasoned round blocks of Parmesan are well known. The fresh, almost milky *mozzarella* is another popular Italian cheese. Dried and cured ham, called *prosciutto*, is a common summer dish in Italy (served with melon slices or figs) that has now traveled across the Atlantic to North America. Specially prepared, high quality olive oil is another important export food from Italy. Pasta, and even fresh pasta, is now a standard part of the European and North American diet. The most famous Italian red wines, such as Chianti and Barolo, are found around the world.

Fast and Slow Food   The tradition of the table in Italy means a large, healthy, and leisurely meal, accompanied by wine and shared by all the family. But the pressures of the modern world are pushing Italians away from this tradition. The culture of "fast food" and the "eat-and-run" attitude have arrived in Italy. It is also more difficult to bring the family all together for a daily meal. Italians have less time to devote to their table, food, wine, and conversation.

But the traditional appreciation of food has sparked a reaction. A new movement endorses the idea of "slow food," which emphasizes the need to take the time to enjoy a meal, to focus on the special regional dishes that make Italian cooking so interesting, to search out the best wines and appreciate their quality, and to dedicate one's attention to the simple pleasures of good food and wine. The Italian traditions of food and the table will probably survive for a long time to come.

Conversation

If there is a national pastime that rivals food in Italy, it must be conversation. The Italians love to talk. They set great store by someone who speaks well and convincingly. Talk is part of the Italians' public and private life. Not only around the family dinner table, but in the bars, in restaurants, on the buses and in the streets, Italians are almost always engaged in animated discussions and often spirited arguments.

There is a second, silent language that accompanies the Italians' words: gestures. The Italians have many ways of expressing an opinion without saying a single word. The shrug of a shoulder, the waving hand, the fingers that trace designs in the air—all of these gestures add considerable emphasis to the conversation. Discussions in Italy often seem to have been choreographed to include these complex signals.

The most common of these gestures is a simple touch. All Italians, young and old, men and women, northerners and southerners, touch each other frequently and openly. Men walk with their arms around each other's shoulders, women stroll hand in hand in the streets, and all Italians greet their friends with a hug and a kiss upon meeting. Indeed, Italians are a people who express their emotions easily, clearly, and publicly. The tenderness and affection expressed through touching, the anger and frustration heard in loud and agitated arguments—

Older Italians pass the day playing cards and talking with friends in a senior citizens' center. Agenzia Fotogiornalistica Cronaca Nuova/Carlo Bozzardi

few emotions are held back in the families and on the streets of Italy. The public display of emotions continues to be a part of Italian cultural tradition, passed down from generation to generation in the family.

Dialects   Talking is a very important aspect of being Italian. But even in their words, Italians reveal the great regional differences that divide the country into many smaller areas. A single language spoken by all people throughout Italy appeared only after the Second World War. What was much more common until the late 1950's were dialects.

Dialects were originally local variations on ancient Latin that over the centuries became almost separate languages. Most often spoken and not written, the dialects are characterized by strong accents, by different pronunciation, and even by different words. They vary immensely from region to region, and in some cases from village to village. In their variety, these "languages" reflect the different cultures of the many areas of Italy. "Official" Italian is itself the version of the Italian language originally spoken only in the region of Tuscany.

Until recently, the first language of most Italians was their local dialect; they "learned Italian" only later, in school. And the Italians continue to use their local dialect within the family and among their friends, reserving "real" Italian only for formal conversations or in their dealings with people from outside of their area.

Dialects are disappearing in Italy. Mandatory education and television have spread the single, official Italian language throughout the country. However, movements to protect the older dialects have appeared in many areas of Italy. The dialects have been written down, and the old songs, peasant proverbs, and folktales have been recorded, all in the hopes of preserving these spoken traces of Italy's earlier history.

The Family

The family is the basic building block of Italian society today. And in contrast to those in many other European and North American countries, the Italian family is still a strong institution. But it is growing smaller. The average size has shrunk over the last forty years, to the current three members. Family size is slightly higher in the more traditional South (3.3) than in the North (2.9).

But whether northern or southern, Italians are simply choosing to have fewer children. Despite the instructions of the Catholic Church, most Italians practice some form of birth control. Today, only 15 percent of Italian families (22 percent in the South and 11 percent in the

North) have five or more members, whereas thirty-five years ago that figure was more than double. The large family, characteristic of rural, peasant Italy, is rapidly disappearing. Fewer children is the most important reason for the decline in population predicted for the twenty-first century.

Family ties are important for modern-day Italians, most of whom remain physically close to their families for their entire lives. It is common for young Italians to attend the university in their own town and to continue to live at home until they marry. Most Italians still choose to live in the same town or the same area as their parents. This creates an extended family in Italy: Both parents and grandparents are actively involved in the upbringing of children. Several generations gather together around the table for the Sunday lunch, for birthdays, and on the major holidays of Easter, Christmas, New Year's, and the Epiphany.

The closeness of the Italian family creates a great sense of stability for its members and acts as a glue holding the larger society together. Respect for others and their opinions is taught early on in the family. A strong moral code, taught by the family and modeled on an older Catholic tradition, encourages responsible social behavior in adult life. As a result, Italy is a remarkably nonviolent society. It has a low crime rate and violent crimes against individuals (except in southern areas where organized crime is active) are rare.

In the past years, the marriage rate has stabilized in Italy. The trend for the future is that the number of Italians who marry will decline and that they will wed at an older age. Increasingly, many younger people in Italy (as elsewhere in the Western world) simply choose to live together rather than formalize their relationship with a marriage. After divorce was legalized in Italy in 1971, the number of divorces grew through the 1980's to a current annual total of over 30,000 (or just under 10 percent of marriages). The divorce rate has now leveled off.

City and Countryside

The pace of daily life in Italy varies enormously from city to countryside. Italy was a country of peasant villages until the late 1950's. Today, about one third of the nation's population still lives in towns with fewer than ten thousand inhabitants, and another one third in cities no larger than fifty thousand people. Life in these areas continues at a slower pace. The small cities and villages are surrounded by open countryside. Town residents, particularly in the small villages, know each other well; the extended family of several generations gathers together frequently.

The larger cities in Italy present a very different picture of daily life. The pace is faster, the countryside far distant, and the city more anonymous. City dwellers are less likely to know their neighbors (though other family members may live nearby). Traffic is heavy and smog is a serious problem. The modern cultural attractions of Italian big cities are few: Rome and Milan, the country's two largest cities, fall far behind other important European cities in contemporary art, cinema, music, and theater. Worst of all, very little has been done over the past decade to face and correct the problems of life in Italy's larger cities.

Some Italians have given up on the city and returned to the countryside, looking for work and a home in some of the medium-sized towns of the provinces. Here, Italians find a simpler way of life, more efficient public services, less congestion, less crowding, and less pollution. Most cities in Italy are now ranked according to their "liveability." Many factors are evaluated in the overall judgment of the quality of life in Italian cities, including the distribution of wealth among the inhabitants, the level of unemployment, the crime rate, and the efficiency of public services. Smaller, provincial towns in the North are almost always at the top of the list; the top five are currently Treviso, Brescia,

Treviso: Italy's Most "Liveable" City

What makes Treviso one of the best places to live in Italy? The following figures (with the national averages listed in parentheses) give some idea:

Population	84,500
Annual Income per Person (lire)	19,700,000 (13,300,000)
Bank Savings per Person (lire)	21,600,000 (10,700,000)
Unemployment	3.3% (12%)
Annual Thefts per 1,000 People	14.2 (26.6)
Museums per 100,000 People	5.9 (2.8)
Sporting Facilities per 100,000 People	15.4 (5.4)

Parma, Perugia, and Bergamo. The larger Italian cities and southern towns are generally found near the bottom. The problems of the urban areas in Italy may continue to encourage Italians out of the cities and back into the countryside.

Whether in cities or the countryside, the Italians remain a highly sociable people whose way of life is based on conversation and interaction. Always together and always talking, the Italians do not have a concept of "privacy"—the word does not exist in their language. Theirs is a public culture, where life is experienced openly, for all to see (and for all to participate in). From the *piazza* to the family, the social life of Italians revolves around contact and communication. And the table, with its food, wine, talk, and family, is still the focal point where most of Italy gathers daily to discuss what is new, old, and in between.

Past, Present, and Future

Modern Italy faces a number of challenges. The country is in the midst of a major transformation, moving away from its traditional peasant roots as it becomes an increasingly modern and urban society. Still the past is there, waiting "around every corner" for the Italians as they think about tomorrow. What does the future hold for a country as profoundly shaped by its past as Italy? How will this country respond to these issues?

Population and Immigration

One of the more important problems is a declining birthrate. Since the days of ancient Rome, Italy has almost always been an overcrowded country, with too many people on its land. This will begin to change to-

Black African immigrants to Italy demanding the end to racism and violent assaults in Florence, 1990. Robert Nossa

ward the end of the twentieth century. If the current birthrate of 1.8 children per couple continues, there will be fewer Italians (perhaps by as many as ten million) in 2020.

Fewer births and fewer young people means that Italy's population will become increasingly older. A shortage of Italians will also mean a need for new workers. One likely source is immigrants to Italy. While these new arrivals may fill the gaps in the work force and help turn around the population decline, their appearance will also create problems.

New peoples will create a multiracial society in Italy. Language, life-style, and even food will change as the new arrivals integrate into Italian society. But the blending of Italian with Asian and African cultures will not be an easy transition in a country that has enjoyed cultural and religious homogeneity for hundreds of years. Incidents of racism can be expected. There have already been some violent attacks on North African immigrants in cities such as Florence. The Italian tradition of tolerance for others, developed over centuries of poverty and overcrowding, will be put to the test by mass immigration. This country's fragile unity will be thoroughly shaken by the appearance of these new peoples.

Regionalism

The regional variations on the peninsula, long a feature in the history of this country, are disappearing in modern Italy. Many factors con-

Newly arrived immigrants have a difficult time finding both work and a home in Italy. Here, they have taken over an abandoned pasta factory in Rome and turned it into a makeshift dormitory. Agenzia Fotogiornalistica Cronaca Nuova/Carlo Bozzardi

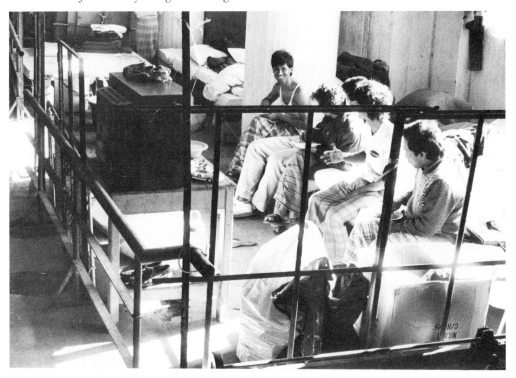

tribute to this change. Economic prosperity has brought greater wealth to even the poorest areas of the South. The television has spread a national language and culture throughout the country. Easier communications, with better roads and the private automobile, have ended the isolation of the mountain and southern areas of Italy. These developments tend to tie together all of Italy's regions.

But the greatest division in Italy—the gap between North and South—remains. There are still substantial economic, social, and cultural differences between these two areas. The Mafia, one of the major barriers to southern development, has to be defeated before law and order can be established in southern Italy. However, the South remains resistant to change and the North unwilling to commit itself fully to answering the "Southern Question." The problems of the South, particularly of organized crime, will grow only more complicated in the meantime.

Though many of the regional barriers will gradually fall, Italians will continue to cherish their local identity. This means that the road to building a national identity is still a long one.

Political Reform

Political reform is another major challenge facing modern Italy. The dynamism of the nation's economy and its society contrast sharply with the immobility of the government. Various reform measures are now proposed to bring the Italian party-ocracy up-to-date. These will institute a more direct democracy in Italy, weaken the network of political patronage, and create the possibility for an alternation in power between the parties of the left and right. Political changes will come slowly to Italy because so many parties have an interest in maintaining the status quo. Reform will also be a delicate undertaking as Italians attempt to make their democratic system more responsive without undermining its greatest strength—the citizens' interest in their country's political affairs.

Italy and the European Economy

The final stage in the establishment of the European Community (EC) is scheduled for the beginning of 1993. People, money, and products of all kinds will be permitted to circulate freely among the Community's twelve member nations. This deadline is another of the challenges facing Italy. Many of the country's problems will have to be solved quickly in order to protect Italy's well-being in this new economic and political climate.

Italy will face open international competition from other countries with more advanced industry, greater technology, and more efficient economies. The typical small shop of Italy may be hard-pressed by this change. The slower pace of business in Italy may be overwhelmed by northern Europeans eager to secure new markets. The inefficient and costly Italian banking system will have to catch up quickly with its competitors. The government subsidies that keep many of Italy's businesses going may be eliminated in the new EC. This move will hit the enormous public sector economy quite heavily. All these changes will require new approaches to the questions of politics and economics in Italy.

The formation of a European economic market will also encourage political change in Italy. More efficient government, greater political stability, and less reliance on patronage are needed to lead Italy into an expanding international economy.

The European Community may also further the process of Italian unification. In order to ensure their position in the multinational

Some young people continue to work at the old peasant crafts of their parents and grandparents. A young man weaving baskets in the Tuscan countryside. Stefania Talini

Community, Italians will have to work hard to defend their own interests. Italy—its people and government—will need to place national interests ahead of regional loyalties. This step could mark the beginnings of a genuine sense of "being Italian," and a major change in outlook for the people of Italy.

Which Way Will the Italians Go?

History offers the Italians few answers to the questions of low birthrate, immigration, regionalism, political reform, and economic renewal. No matter how urgent the problems, new solutions will no doubt come slowly to Italy.

The weight of this country's history is just too heavy to allow the

Italians rapidly to change their lives. Traditional ways have stood the test of time and are familiar and reassuring. This makes the Italians hesitant to adopt new ideas or approaches too quickly.

The Italians are somewhat suspicious of the concept of "change." The centuries of history and all the developments in their past make it hard for them to believe in the idea of anything really "new." Rather, as one Sicilian novelist wrote, the Italians maintain that "everything changes in order to remain the same."

All this means that even the most pressing challenges of the present in Italy will eventually be solved, but only in an Italian manner: Gradual change, and not a sharp break with the past, will characterize the Italian way of facing the country's problems.

Old Traditions in a Modern Society

Strong ties to the past are still evident in modern Italy. Old rituals and ceremonies continue today, giving people a sense of participation in their community and of belonging to their past.

One of the best known of these traditions is the summer horse races in Siena. In July and again in August, ten neighborhoods in this small city each choose a horse and jockey to race three times around the main *piazza* in a contest called the *Palio*. At stake is the prestige and importance of the tiny neighborhood (though a great amount of money is bet as well). Jockey and horse are blessed in the church of their neighborhood in the early morning. All the contenders then parade around Siena's main square in historic costumes. The enthusiasm and excitement mount as the race time of 7:30 P.M. approaches, reaching hysterical levels as the horses begin to run. The first to finish takes home the prize.

Summer celebrations in Siena's main *piazza* go back almost a thousand years. Originally a religious ceremony to honor the Virgin Mary,

The Palio in Siena. Each neighborhood sponsors a horse and jockey, competing for the honor of the city in a race that dates back to the 1200's. ENIT, Roma

The new year begins in Rome with a daring dive into the polluted waters of the Tiber River. Mr. Bandini made his last plunge in 1987 at 75 years of age. A younger man now carries on the tradition. Agenzia Fotogiornalistica Cronaca Nuova/Carlo Bozzardi

the *Palio* acquired a political tone in 1260 in celebration of Siena's victory over its rival city-state, Florence. Horse racing became the official conclusion to the ceremony in the mid-1600's. Today, the people of Siena have made their race into a major tourist attraction (broadcast on Italian television), but its real meaning remains that of the pride and independence of a tiny hilltop town.

Age-old rituals are common elsewhere. Each July, the people of Venice celebrate the end of the great plague that devastated their city in the fourteenth century. Also in Venice, but later in September, the city holds its "Grand Regatta." The oldest and most magnificent gondolas take to the canals in celebration of the glory of the Venetian Empire five hundred years ago. In the capital of Italy, the Romans still take a day off from work on April 21 to mark the foundation of their

Each April 21, Romans observe the birthday of their city (in 753 B.C.) with traditional celebrations in front of the City Hall and a day off work. Agenzia Fotogiornalistica Cronaca Nuova/Carlo Bozzardi

city in 753 B.C. In Sardinia, when a dry spell threatens crops, the people turn to old peasant rituals and pray to pre-Christian gods for rain.

What does it mean to be an Italian? It means to be connected to the past and over three thousand years of continuous civilization, and to live in a modern, Western society surrounded by the ruins of those ancient times. It means strong ties to the family, to a town, and to a region, to feel secure in the present because of firm roots in the past. Modern-day Italy is a country that never escapes the weight of its history even as it flourishes day by day.

Bibliography

History and Society

Arlacchi, Pino. *Mafia Business*. New York: Verso, 1987. The Mafia and its criminal
activities seen in terms of its economic and social function in southern Italy.

Barzini, Luigi. *The Italians*. New York: Bantam, 1965. A book that is really an
extended essay on the Italians, their society, and their outlook on the world.

Blinkhorn, Martin. *Mussolini and Fascist Italy*. London: Methuen, 1984. A very read-
able introduction to the man and the Fascist movement.

Block, Anton. *The Mafia of a Sicilian Village, 1860–1960*. London: Oxford, 1974. A
very good historical study of how the Mafia developed and worked.

Bondanella, Peter. *Italian Cinema: From Neorealism to the Present*. New York:
Ungar, 1985. The best presentation of the films and directors of the post-war
Italian cinema.

Clark, Martin. *Modern Italy, 1871–1982*. New York, Longman: 1984. An overview of
Italian history from unification, the book suffers from an institutional focus that
makes it slow reading.

Cunningham, Lawrence, and John Reich. *Culture and Values: A Survey of Western Humanities* (2 volumes). Fort Worth: Holt, Rinehart and Winston, 1990. A survey of Western art and culture, with particularly good chapters on ancient Rome and Renaissance Italy. Excellent introductory discussions of the works of art.

Francis, Saint. *The Little Flowers of St. Francis.* Raphael Brown, translator. New York: Doubleday, 1958. The writings of St. Francis.

Ginsborg, Paul. *A History of Contemporary Italy: Society and Politics, 1943–1988.* London: Viking Penguin, 1990. The best and the most recent study of Italian history from the Second World War to the present, particularly sensitive to the changes in society.

Gooch, John. *The Unification of Italy.* London: Methuen, 1986. A short, very good pamphlet that traces the history and important figures of the period from 1815 to 1870.

Hay, Denys. *The Italian Renaissance in Its Historical Background.* New York: Cambridge, 1981. A general discussion of the Renaissance philosophy, spirit, and accomplishments in Italy.

Hebblethwaite, Peter. *In the Vatican.* New York: Oxford, 1986. Probably the best discussion of the Vatican and the papacy of John Paul II.

LaPalombara, Joseph. *Democracy: Italian Style.* New Haven, CT: Yale University Press, 1987. An enthusiastic introduction to the politics of contemporary Italy that overlooks many of the system's serious shortcomings.

Mack-Smith, Denis. *Italy: A Modern History*, rev. and enl. ed. Ann Arbor, MI: University of Michigan Press, 1969. The standard history text for the period from the 1800's through World War II written by the foremost English historian of Italy.

————. *Mussolini: a Political Biography.* New York: Random, 1982. The best account of Mussolini, full of insights into the Duce's personality and the Fascist movement.

————. *Garibaldi: A Great Life in Brief.* Westport, CT: Greenwood Press, 1982. Part of the Great Lives series, this short book is a fine introduction to the life and historical contributions of Garibaldi.

————. *Cavour and Garibaldi. 1860: A Study of Political Conflict.* New York: Cambridge, 1985. Fascinating account of the two men—and the relations between them— who "made" unified Italy in the late 1850's and early 1860's.

————. *Italy and Its Monarchy.* New Haven, CT: Yale University Press, 1989. The history of the kings of Italy from unification to the Republic.

Moorman, John. *St. Francis of Assisi.* London: SPCK, 1979. The biography of the rich man who chose poverty in the name of religious service.

Procacci, Giuliano. *A History of the Italian People.* New York: Viking Penguin, 1986. An excellent and brief introduction to Italy from the tenth century to the present.

Spotts, Frederic, and Theodor Wieser. *Italy: A Difficult Democracy*. New York: Cambridge, 1986. The best introduction to the politics and institutions of contemporary Italy.

Sefarty, Simon, and Lawrence Grey, editors. *The Italian Communist Party: Yesterday, Today and Tomorrow*. Westport, CT: Greenwood Press, 1980. The history and status of the Italian Communist Party prior to the recent re-formation.

Stambaugh, John. *The Ancient Roman City*. Baltimore: Johns Hopkins University Press, 1988. Describes the daily life and cityscape of Rome at the peak of its ancient power.

Woolf, Stuart. *A History of Italy, 1700–1860: The Social Constraints of Political Change*. London: Methuen, 1979. The best book on the history of Italy up to unification.

Ziegler, Philip. *The Black Death*. New York: Harper & Row, 1969. A very good, short introduction to the Black Death—its origins, spread through Europe, and effect on European peoples, culture, and civilization.

Zuccotti, Susan. *The Italians and the Holocaust*. New York: Basic, 1987. A useful, though simple, introduction to the Jews in Italy and their fate during the late 1930's and early 1940's.

Literature

Dante Alighieri. *The Divine Comedy*. Three volumes: *Inferno, Purgatory, Paradise*. New York: Penguin, 1984–86. One of the masterpieces of Italian literature from the thirteenth century.

Guareschi, Giovanni. *The Little World of Don Camillo*. New York: Doubleday, 1986. A Communist mayor and a Catholic priest clash and cooperate in an Emilian village in the 1950's.

Lampedusa, Giuseppe di. *The Leopard*. New York: Pantheon, 1960. A magnificent description of what unification meant for the island of Sicily from 1860 to the early 1900's.

Levi, Carlo. *Christ Stopped at Eboli*. New York: Farrar, Straus and Giroux, 1981. Rural southern society of the 1930's seen through the eyes of an opponent to Mussolini.

Levi, Primo. *The Periodic Table*. New York: Shocken, 1986. Reflections on life in Italy from the 1920's to the 1950's.

Lewis, Norman. *Naples '44*. New York: Pantheon, 1978. Allied-occupied Naples during the war.

Mann, Thomas. "Mario and the Magician" in *A Death in Venice and Other Stories*. New York: Bantam, 1988. An excellent short story by one of Europe's great writers. The subject is Fascism and mass hypnosis, and the setting is a Romagna seaside resort in the late 1920's.

Manzoni, Alessandro. *The Betrothed*. New York: Penguin, 1984. Italy's first "historical" novel, about life in Milan toward the end of the 1700's.

Newby, Eric. *Love and War in the Apennines*. New York, Viking Penguin, 1990. During World War II, an English prisoner of war escapes into the Emilian hills and lives among the peasants.

Pavese, Cesare. *The Moon and the Bonfire*. New York: Quartet Books, 1978. An Italian immigrant to America returns to his home village soon after the end of the Second World War and tries to make sense of his memories and recent experiences abroad.

Pirandello, Luigi. *Naked Masks*. New York: Dutton, 1952. Five of Pirandello's best known plays, including *Six Characters in Search of an Author*, translated into English.

Sciascia, Leonardo. *The Day of the Owl-Equal Danger*. New York: Godine, 1983. An investigator tries to solve a Mafia murder and discovers the extent of the Mafia's connections in a small southern village.

Silone, Ignazio. *Bread and Wine*. New York: Signet, 1963. A Communist tries to inspire opposition to Fascism among the peasants of the Abruzzi Mountains and discovers much about himself in the process.

Filmography

Feature Films

There are scores of Italian films documenting the history of the country since the Second World War. This is only a partial list of some of the more popular feature films with a historical or social slant. Most of these films are available in Italian with English subtitles; some, however, are dubbed into English.

Amarcord. Federico Fellini (1974). The most "historical" of Fellini's films, this focuses on life in a small provincial town in Romagna during Fascism.

L'Avventura. Michelangelo Antonioni (1960). The loneliness of life in Italy during the transformation from a rural to an agrarian society.

The Bicycle Thief. Vittorio De Sica (1948). A classic of neorealism, this film shows the very difficult conditions facing the Italians immediately after the conclusion of World War II.

Bitter Rice. Giuseppe De Santis (1949–50). Another film that defined the neorealist style, it depicts the life of women workers in the rice fields in the early 1950's.

Bread and Chocolate. Franco Brusati (1973). The lives of Italian emigrants in Switzerland in the 1970's are used to contrast the two societies.

Christ Stopped at Eboli. Francesco Rosi (1979). The film explores southern society as seen through the eyes of a political opponent to Fascism exiled into the Basilicata in the 1930's.

Cinema Paradiso. Giuseppe Tornatori (1988). Winner of an Academy Award in 1990, this is a film about movies and moviegoers in a small southern town in the 1950's and 1960's.

La Dolce Vita. Federico Fellini (1959). Here we are shown glimpses of the lives of the rich and beautiful during the early years of Italy's economic miracle.

The Family. Ettore Scola (1987). The Italian family through three generations in the twentieth century.

The Garden of the Finzi-Continis. Vittorio De Sica (1970). The film focuses on Italian Jews in the Emilian city of Ferrara during the years of Fascism.

The Icicle Thief. Maurizio Nichetti (1988). Though the title is a play on the 1948 De Sica classic, this film has a different story: the collision of two cultures in Italy, one tied to the war and one tied to a modern consumerist society.

The Leopard. Luchino Visconti (1963). The film version of Lampedusa's breathtaking novel about Sicily in the 1860's and 1870's.

Miracle in Milan. Vittorio De Sica (1950). The director presents a fantasy story about the lives and dreams of Milan's poor in the late 1940's.

The Night of the Shooting Stars. Taviani Brothers (1985). A young girl remembers the Second World War in a small Tuscan village.

1900. Bernardo Bertolucci (1975–76). The director presents an epic history of Italy over the first forty-five years of the twentieth century.

The Organizer. Mario Monicelli (1963). This film dramatically shows the problems facing workers in Italy's earliest industrial cities.

Padre Padrone. Taviani Brothers (1977). Rural life in backward Sardinia.

Paisan. Roberto Rossellini (1946). We are shown five short episodes about the war in Italy, 1943–1945.

Rocco and His Brothers. Luchino Visconti (1960). The lives of a southern family moved north during the 1950's.

Roma. Federico Fellini (1971). The director pays homage to the city, its people, its wonders, and problems.

Rome, Open City. Roberto Rossellini (1945). A landmark film in the neorealist style treats the Resistance in Rome in 1943–1944.

Swept Away . . . Lina Wertmüller (1974). This film is a spoof of traditional sex roles, social classes, and the differences between the North and South in Italy.

The Tree of the Wooden Clogs. Ermanno Olmi (1978). Peasant society in northern Italy around the turn of the century.

Most of these films are available on videocassette. Alternatively, there are many North American distributors for these films. Two of the best stocked are:

Films Incorporated
440 Park Avenue South
New York, NY 10016
or
5625 Hollywood Boulevard
Hollywood, CA 90028

Cinema 5
1500 Broadway
New York, NY 10036

The best source for printed, visual, and audio information on Italy is the national tourist office of the Italian government. Contact the Italian Government Travel Office (ENIT) at any of these locations:

Suite 1565
630 5th Avenue
New York, NY 10020
Tel: (212) 245-4822
Fax: (212) 586-9249

Suite 801
360 Post Street
San Francisco, CA 94108
Tel: (415) 392-6206
Fax: (415) 392-6852

Suite 1046
500 N. Michigan Avenue
Chicago, IL 60611
Tel: (312) 644-0990
Fax: (312) 392-6852

Educational Films

The Italian Institute of Culture is an excellent source of videotapes, films, and audio-visual material for noncommercial organizations and institutions. Some of the film categories include archaeology, architecture, cinema, history, language, literature, music and dance, science, and industry. The Institute also has a newsreel collection, and all materials are available free of charge. For further information and a catalog, contact The Italian Institute of Culture, 686 Park Avenue, New York, NY 10021.

Documentaries

Bill Moyers's "The Power of the Past: Florence." Part of a series produced by the Public Broadcasting Service, this one-hour special explores the Italian Renaissance and includes interesting discussion by leading experts in Italian art, literature, and history.

Discography

Current popular performers in Italy whose recordings are available in North America include Lucio Dalla, Pino Daniele, Mina, Gianna Nannini, Ornella Vanoni, and Antonello Venditti.

A wide range of Italian opera and classical music is available on record, cassette, and compact disc. The work of most of the major opera singers and orchestral conductors from Italy can also be easily found.

A musical style known as *cantautori*, whose balladlike songs are written, composed, and sung by one person, is also very popular. This music is available primarily in collections and can be obtained through local record stores.

Additionally, there are a number of recordings of folk and protest songs as well as collections of songs from the Resistance period, all available on records and cassette tapes.

Index

Numbers in *italics* refer to illustrations.